INSULATION AND DAMP-PROOFING

TIME
LIFE
BOOKS

This volume is part of a series offering home
owners detailed instructions on repairs,
construction and improvements which they can
undertake themselves.

HOME REPAIR
AND IMPROVEMENT

INSULATION AND DAMP-PROOFING

BY THE EDITORS OF
TIME-LIFE BOOKS

TIME-LIFE BOOKS
AMSTERDAM

TIME-LIFE BOOKS

EUROPEAN EDITOR: Kit van Tulleken
Design Director: Ed Skyner
Photography Director: Pamela Marke
Chief of Research: Vanessa Kramer
Chief Sub-Editor: Ilse Gray

HOME REPAIR AND IMPROVEMENT

EDITORIAL STAFF FOR INSULATION AND DAMP-PROOFING
Editor: William Frankel
Assistant Editors: Edward Brash, Lee Hassig
Designer: Herbert H. Quarmby
Picture Editor: Kay Neil Noble
Associate Designer: Robert McKee
Text Editor: Gerry Schremp
Staff Writers: Jane Alexander, Helen Barer, Marilyn
Bethany, Sally French, Simone D. Gossner, Lee Greene,
Michael Luftman, Brian McGinn, Joan Mebane, James
Murphy, Don Nelson
Art Associates: Richard Salcer, Victoria Vebell, Mary B.
Wilshire
Editorial Assistant: Eleanor G. Kask

EUROPEAN EDITION
Project Director: Jackie Matthews
Editors: Tony Allan, Christopher Farman
Researchers: Margaret Hall, Deirdre McGarry, Judith
Perle
Designers: Cherry Doyle, Paul Reeves
Sub-Editors: Charles Boyle, Sally Rowland

EDITORIAL PRODUCTION
Chief: Ellen Brush
Production Assistants: Stephanie Lee, Jane Lillicrap
Art Department: Janet Matthew
Editorial Department: Theresa John, Debra Lelliott

ISBN 7054 0785 3

THE CONSULTANTS: Richard Westacott has been working in the field of
general construction, home repair, refurbishment and improvement for
nearly two decades. He has written numerous articles and publications,
as well as participated on local and national radio programmes, on the
problems of home improvement and house maintenance.

Rex Holme, a director of Pattison Insulations Limited, one of the largest
insulation and draughtproofing contractors in the U.K., has 30 years'
experience in the building industry. He is chairman of the National
Association of Loft Insulation Contractors and is a member of the
Draughtproofing Advisory Association.

Lelland L. Gallup is Assistant Professor of Housing and Design at New
York State College of Human Ecology, Cornell University, Ithaca, New
York. He is responsible for a series of innovative home-maintenance
courses given to New York state home owners and home associations, and
has written numerous articles on home repair.

Contents

Keeping a House Snug and Tight

Above all else, a house is built to provide shelter for its occupants from the elements. To protect the house against intrusion by draughts and water, heat and cold—even fungi and insects—is a principal concern of the home owner. This continuous battle against the elements is fought with a varied arsenal of materials and equipment. There are plugs and sealers, fans and vents, insulation, awnings and tinted plastics—plus a range of special treatments for houses which have already been damaged by the intrusion of water.

Few houses demand every weatherproofing remedy in this book, but sooner or later most require one or more of them to remain sound and comfortable. Every few years, for example, new caulking around the frames of doors and windows and perhaps new weatherstripping are needed to replace materials that have worn out and to seal up gaps that appear as the house settles. Once it is properly sealed, a house may have too little air entering to carry moisture away or to keep the boiler burning efficiently. Therefore, ventilators must be installed that take advantage of natural air currents or that create their own with electric ventilating fans. Intentional ventilation of this sort has a major advantage over the accidental air currents that come through odd cracks and crannies in the house; it allows you to control exactly how much air gets in and where it does so.

Although ventilation removes airborne moisture, other measures are necessary to cure a house of leaks. In many houses, the basement, ground floor walls or the floor itself may be affected by damp. In some cases, the solution to problems of damp may be as simple as cleaning out the gutters to improve the drainage of rainwater, or sealing cracks in foundation walls or leaks in the roof. When such routine steps are insufficient, you may have to lay underground pipe to carry water away, perhaps to a soakaway, or you may want to apply waterproofing to the foundation walls, or install a damp-proof course.

Another kind of seepage has nothing to do with water but exacts a toll in money and comfort. In summer, heat entering the house through the walls, roof, basement, doors and windows can considerably increase the running costs of an air-conditioning system. In winter, heat escapes from the house by the same routes—and, as energy prices continue to rise, such a loss has become intolerably expensive. Depending on where you live, your house will benefit from at least 100 mm of insulation in the attic, for example, and double glazing for the windows—a form of insulation that you can build as well as install yourself—is a necessity in all but the mildest climates as a finishing touch in making your house impervious to the elements.

Weatherstripping to Block the Draughts

A house can lose up to 15 per cent of its heat through draughts—caused mainly by the gaps around doors and windows. The illustrations here and on pages 10–15 will show you how to overcome the problem by installing your own weatherstripping.

There are some simple tests to determine your weatherstripping needs. On a cool, windy day, feel for draughts by holding your hand over several places along the edges of doors and windows. Alternatively, hold a tissue next to the edge to see if it flutters. Another method is to shine a torch along door and window edges from the outside at night while someone inside watches to see if the light penetrates.

Once you have identified the trouble spots, you can select the weatherstripping best suited to the job. Although strips are available in a wide variety of materials and designs (below), they can be divided into two main types: the "compression" strips, which are squeezed between a unit and its frame, and the "wiping" strips, which are usually attached to a moving door or window and are larger than the gap they block. Some strips come with a self-adhesive backing and can be applied to both wooden and metal frames, others must be nailed or screwed into place and are suitable only for wooden frames. As an alternative to weatherstripping, you can use a silicone rubber sealant which is squeezed from a caulking gun (overleaf).

Before installing weatherstripping, particularly the self-adhesive type, make sure that the surfaces are dry and free from dust, dirt or grease, and make good any patches of flaking paint. Silicone sealants may require special primers—follow the manufacturer's instructions.

You should also check that the doors and windows are working properly. (When installing weatherstripping, do not make the seals too tight or windows and doors will not open smoothly.) Doors that do not hang straight may have to be shimmed to eliminate sticking (page 13). Sometimes sash windows will not shut all the way: the top rail of the lower sash and the bottom rail of the upper sash should meet evenly across the centre of the window. If they do not, scrape paint or dirt off top and bottom rails and their channels. It may be necessary to sand the window.

An effective seal for sash windows is provided by the spring metal strips shown on these pages. Such strips (also available in plastic) are only nailed along one edge; the other edge springs out to contact the closing edge of the window. The strips are invisible when the window is closed.

Any of the types shown below, as well as silicone sealants, are suitable for casement windows. Brush strips, which must be mounted in full view, are ideal for sliding windows, where friction between the surfaces may cause other types of weatherstripping to work loose.

A Choice of Materials

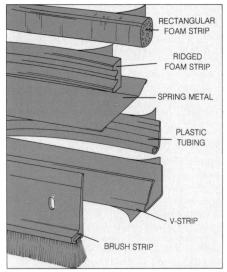

RECTANGULAR FOAM STRIP

RIDGED FOAM STRIP

SPRING METAL

PLASTIC TUBING

V-STRIP

BRUSH STRIP

Selecting weatherstripping. Durable spring metal is hidden when doors or windows are shut. Self-adhesive foam strips are cheap and easy to install, but may work loose on movable surfaces. Ridged foam strips seal uneven gaps more effectively than rectangular strips. V-strips press against the closing edge of a door or window. Plastic tubing is fixed to the frame so that when shut the door or window presses against the flexible tube at the edge of the strip. Brush strips are durable and easy to install, but are more obtrusive than other types. Silicone sealant (overleaf) produces a tailor-made seal especially effective for uneven gaps.

Spring Metal for Sash Windows

UPPER SASH

LOWER SASH

1 **Measuring the strips.** On sash windows, spring metal weatherstripping is installed in the side channels of both upper and lower sashes, on the bottom rails of the upper and lower sashes and on the top rail of the upper sash.

To determine the length of the four side channel strips, raise the lower sash, then measure from the base of one channel to a point 50 mm above the bottom rail of the upper sash. Use a sturdy pair of scissors to cut the strips. Finally, measure the bottom rail of the lower sash and cut three strips of the same length.

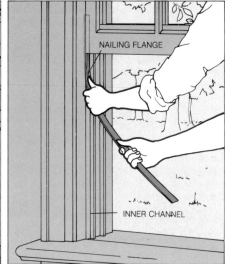

NAILING FLANGE

INNER CHANNEL

2 **Installing bottom-sash channel strips.** Each metal strip must be installed so the nailing flange lies flush against the inside edge of the frame. Open the lower sash as far as possible and remove any loose paint or dirt from the channels. Slip the end of a strip into the narrow slit between sash and channel, and slide the strip upwards until it fills the bottom of the inner channel. Repeat on the other side. If you cannot readily slip the strips into place, scrape out the slits with a thin-bladed knife and try again.

3 Securing the channel strips. Fasten the strips by nailing through the indentations near the edge. Secure the lower portion of the lower-sash channel strips first; then drop the lower sash and fasten the portion that extends above the top rail.

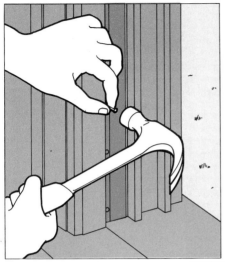

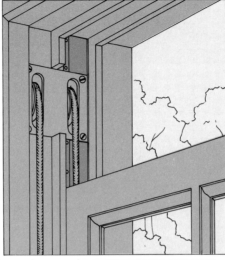

4 Installing outer-channel strips. If the window lacks rope or chain pulleys, lower both sashes as far as possible and install strips in the tops of the outer channels as you did in the bottoms of the inner channels (Steps 2 and 3).

If the window has pulleys, as shown here, proceed as follows. Cut the metal into two pieces—one to fit above the pulley and one to extend from the pulley to a point 50 mm below the top rail of the lower sash. Install the piece above the pulley, and fasten extra nails across its bottom edge. With the top and bottom sashes still all the way down, pull the rope or chain out of the way and feed the long strip into the outer channel below the pulley. Nail the strip in place, then push both sashes all the way up and fasten the end that protrudes below the upper sash's bottom rail.

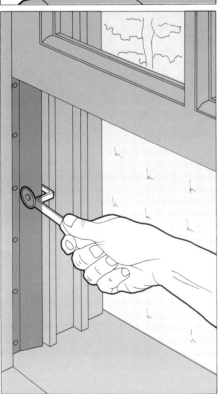

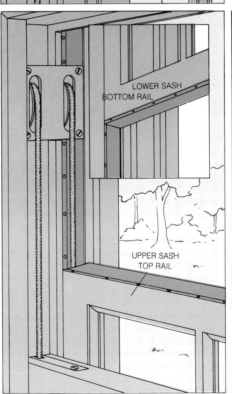

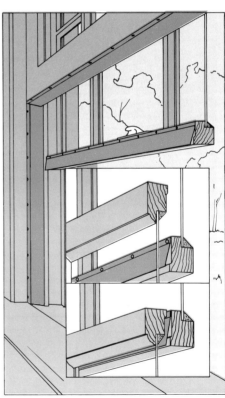

LOWER SASH BOTTOM RAIL

UPPER SASH TOP RAIL

5 Tightening the seal. Once the channel strips are nailed in place, use a special springing tool to bend out the unfastened side about 5 mm, or until the window holds position but does not stick. Run the wheel of the tool along the springing line next to the nails and lift up the outer edge of the strip with the projecting part of the tool (above). The greater the pressure you apply to the wheel, the more the free side of the metal strip will spring out—and the tighter the seal will be.

6 Installing top and bottom cross strips. Metal strips should extend across the full width of the window on the top side of the top rail of the upper sash, and also on the underside of the bottom rail of the bottom sash. The flange to be nailed should be positioned along the inside edge of the window. (Hammer gently or you may crack the glass.) Once in place, prise out the two crosspieces as shown in Step 5.

7 Mounting the centre cross strip. Install the last metal strip on the inner side of the bottom rail of the upper sash (above). The nailing flange should extend across the top edge of the rail. After fastening the strip, sink the nails well into the metal by hammering them again with a nail set; this will ensure that the sashes move smoothly yet maintain a tight seal when closed (inset). Complete the installation by bending this strip as you have the others.

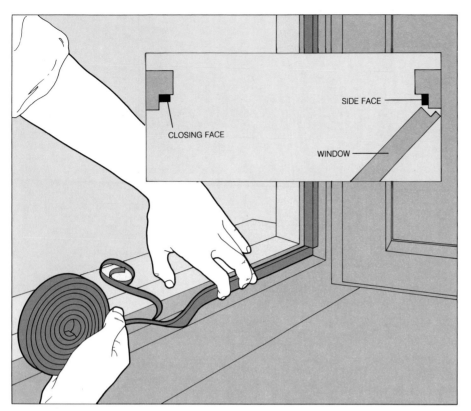

Foam Strip for Casement Windows

Installing the strip. Press the adhesive side of each strip directly into the frame rebate, slowly peeling off the protective backing as you do so. The diagram *(inset)* shows where the foam should be placed on the side and closing faces of the window. Cut the foam with a utility knife or scissors when you reach a corner of the frame or the window catch or hinges. At corners, simply abut the adjacent strips; foam is compressible and need not be mitred.

CLOSING FACE

SIDE FACE

WINDOW

A Sealant for All Surfaces

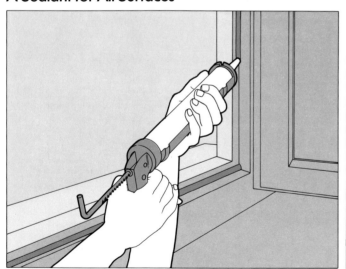

1 Caulking a bead of sealant. Prime aluminium and galvanized steel surfaces first, following the instructions on the sealant cartridge. With a caulking gun, apply a continuous bead of sealant to the side and closing faces of the window rebate *(above)*, using the technique described on page 18. To allow for compression of the sealant, cut the nozzle of the cartridge to give a bead slightly thicker than the gap to be filled. Avoid caulking over the hinges and window catch.

2 Applying a release agent. To prevent the freshly applied sealant from sticking to the opening part of the window, apply a release agent to those areas that will come into contact with the sealant when the window is shut. Brush on a thin film of high-quality washing-up liquid *(above)*. Alternatively, use petroleum jelly or masking tape. Take care not to damage the sealant. Close the window and wait for the sealant to harden—this usually takes from one to two days. Then open the window carefully and wash or peel off the release agent. If necessary, trim the sealant bead with a sharp utility knife.

Plastic Tubing for Casement Windows

Fixing plastic tube. Apply the vertical sides first. Measure and cut the plastic tubing to length and, if it is self-adhesive, peel off about 200 mm of backing paper. Starting at the top of the window, press the strip to the frame, making sure that the tube protrudes over the edge of the frame. Work down the frame, applying gentle pressure to the strip and removing the backing paper as you proceed. Along the top and bottom of the frame, position the strip so that the tube points downwards and upwards respectively *(inset)*. To ensure a permanent, tight seal, pin the plastic tubing along its flat edge *(right)*.

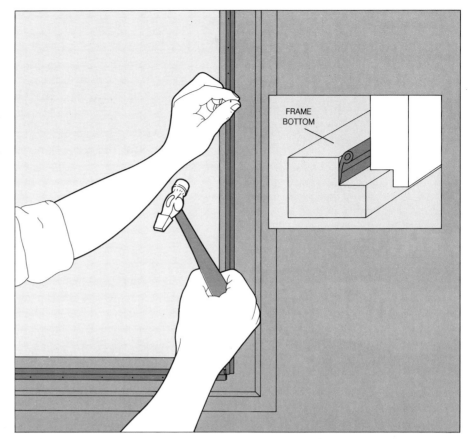

FRAME BOTTOM

Sliding Windows

Draught-proofing sliding windows. Most modern sliding windows are already weatherproofed. Older types, however, may need to be sealed. If both parts of the window move, treat it as if it were a sash window turned on its side. For windows with only one sliding sash *(right)*, treat only the movable part.

Fix brush strips to the top and bottom of the sliding sash so that the brush points towards the window frame. Whether you do this on the inside or the outside depends on the construction of the window—in the drawing on the right it is the inner sash that moves and therefore weather-stripping is installed on the inside of the window. Also fix a brush strip to the meeting rail of the movable sash so that the brush points towards the meeting rail of the fixed sash. Along the vertical edge of the frame that receives the sliding sash you can either use brush strip fixed to the frame so that the brush points towards the sliding sash, or self-adhesive foam or V-strip fixed into the side rebate. Always position the brush strip so that it gently presses against the opposite surface.

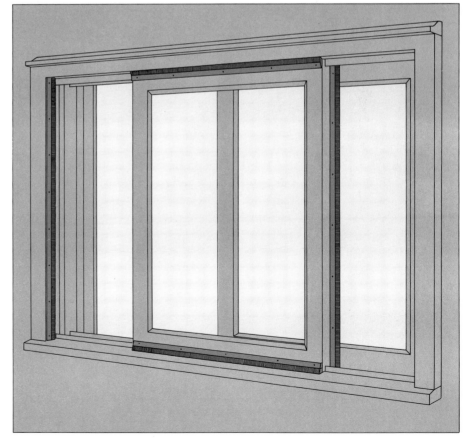

Weatherstripping Doors

Various types of weatherstripping are available for sealing a door against draughts, but none will do so effectively unless the door itself fits properly. Indeed, if weatherstripping is attached to a door that sticks, it may prevent the door from opening or closing.

A careful inspection will usually show exactly where a door edge is sticking. If it does not, slide a piece of thin cardboard between the closed door and the frame, and note where the cardboard sticks. Alternatively, rub coloured chalk along the door edge, then close the door—the chalk will rub off on the frame at the places where the door is sticking.

Most often a door sticks because the hinge screws have become loose and are causing it to sag. Tightening the screws should correct the fault. If the screws will not hold, remove them, insert wall plugs into the holes and then refit the screws.

If a door sticks and you can find nothing wrong with the hinges, it may be that part of the door has swollen. In that case, the easiest solution is to fit shims under one of the hinge leaves so that you bring the swollen part of the door away from the frame *(opposite page, above)*. Where swelling is severe, however, you will have to plane off the excess. If the entire latch side sticks, remove the door completely and plane down the hinge side, which is easier than leaving the door in place and removing the lock in order to plane the latch side.

Once you have fixed the door so that it operates smoothly, select one of the weatherstripping materials illustrated below to close the gaps at the sides and top. The gap at the bottom of the door is sealed differently, using one of the devices described overleaf. For weatherstripping sliding doors, follow the instructions given for sliding windows *(page 11)*.

Types of weatherstripping. Most durable and effective of weatherstrippings is the so-called V-strip. A doubled-over strip of springy plastic, it fits on the door stop's inner face, filling the crack between door and frame. Less expensive are vinyl-sheathed strips of foam or rubber backed with adhesive. Also fitted between door edge and frame, they are available in two forms: square for general use, or with ridged surfaces for use where gaps are uneven. Other types of weatherstripping are attached to the side of the door stop so that their flexible edges press against the door face when it is closed. The sturdiest and least obtrusive of these types are metal or plastic strips, edged with nylon brush or plastic tubing, which look like decorative trim.

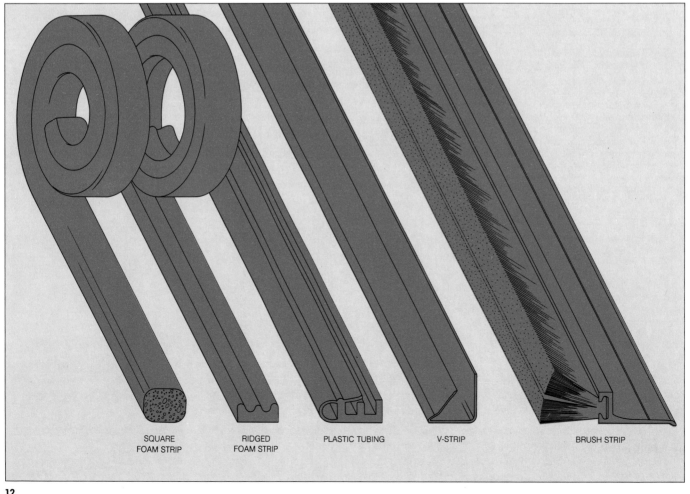

SQUARE FOAM STRIP   RIDGED FOAM STRIP   PLASTIC TUBING   V-STRIP   BRUSH STRIP

Straightening a door. If the top or bottom edge of the door sticks, plane or sand that edge until the door fits easily. If a door sticks on its leading edge—where the lock is installed—you may be able to solve the problem by inserting a thin shim of wood or plastic under the jamb leaf of one hinge. Wedge a piece of wood under the bottom of the door for support, unscrew the leaf and add shims until the sticking is eliminated. If a door sticks near the top of the leading edge, shim out the lower hinge; if it sticks lower down, shim out the upper hinge. For doors that stick on the hinge side, shim out the hinge that is nearest the sticking place.

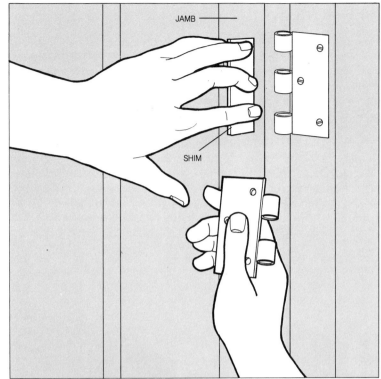

Installing V-strip weatherstripping. Cut strips to run along both sides and the top of the door stop's inner face: the edge against which the door closes. Trim away sections to allow for the lock and the hinges, and mitre one end of each vertical strip and both ends of the top strip so that abutting strips will form a neat right angle. With the point of the V facing the door, fix each strip to the frame *(below)*.

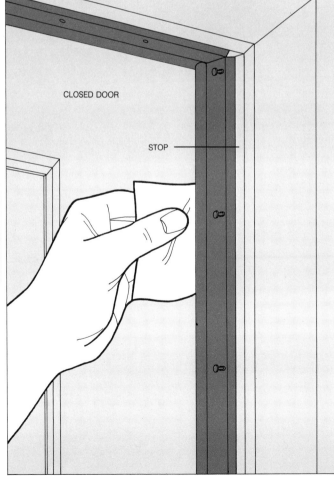

Attaching external weatherstripping. Cut strips to run along both sides and the top of the door stop moulding. Working from the outside of the door with the door closed, position the top strip against the top stop, pressing the flexible edge lightly against the door face. Attach the strip to the stop with nails or screws, but do not drive them all the way in. Install the side strips in the same way. Use a piece of paper to test the positioning of the top and side strips: the space between the door and the flexible edge should be barely sufficient to slide in the paper. Adjust strip positions and fixings as necessary, then drive the fixings all the way in.

Seals for the Bottom

External doors should always be sealed, and the weatherstripping should be fixed to the inside face. If you want to keep some rooms in the house at a higher temperature than others, seal internal doors as well; attach the strip to either face. A number of weatherstripping devices are available, enabling you to plug even the most troublesome gap.

Plain threshold strips *(below, left)* drag a flexible length of rubber or plastic, or a nylon brush, held in an aluminium or plastic carrier, against the sill or floor, and are suitable for both internal and external doors. Threshold brush strips are recommended for sliding doors, since other types of weatherstripping may prevent the doors from opening and closing smoothly. Some brush strips designed for external doors incorporate a plastic fin inside the brush that helps prevent rainwater from penetrating.

A variation of the plain threshold strip, known as a combination strip *(below, centre)*, comes in two parts—a nylon brush strip for the door and metal strip (sometimes called a bottom bearer) for the sill. If the inside face of the door is flush with the sill—as shown below—the metal strip will provide a surface for the brush strip to press against. And if the sill has become so worn that it dips in the middle, the metal strip will bridge the hollow.

The outside face of external doors should always be protected by a weather bar *(below, right)*, a length of timber or aluminium that is shaped to deflect rainwater from the bottom of the door. A groove that runs underneath the weather bar prevents water from seeping back into the sill.

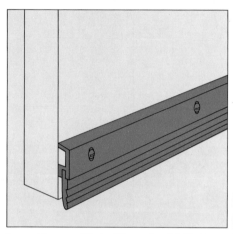
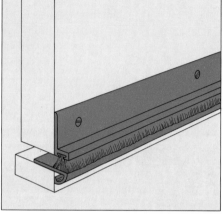
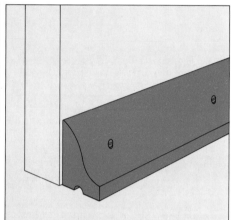

Installing a Plain Threshold Strip

Fixing the strip. Cut the strip to the width of the door and screw or nail it across the bottom of the door so that it fits snugly against the floor or sill when the door is shut, yet allows the door to open and close smoothly. Many threshold strips have slots, so positioning is easily adjusted.

Installing a Combination Strip

1 **Fixing the metal sill strip.** Cut both the sill and the door strips to the exact width of the sill. Then screw the sill strip in place, making sure that the overhanging edge of the strip faces the inside of the door opening.

2 **Securing the brush door strip.** With the door closed and the bristles of the brush strip gently pressing against the sill strip, screw or nail the brush strip across the inside bottom face of the door.

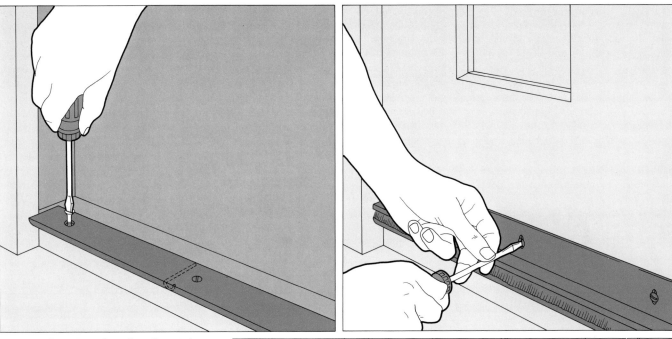

A Weather Bar for the Outside

Fixing the bar. Cut the weather bar to the exact width of the door and position it so that the door opens and closes smoothly. The bottom of the bar should lie flush with, or a couple of millimetres above, the bottom edge of the door. With the door closed, fasten the weather bar to the outside face with screws or nails. Use galvanized nails or screws to avoid rusting.

For extra protection, use a caulking gun to fill the crack between the top of the weather bar and the surface of the door with a narrow bead of mastic sealant. This will prevent water from penetrating between the two and causing the bottom of the door to rot.

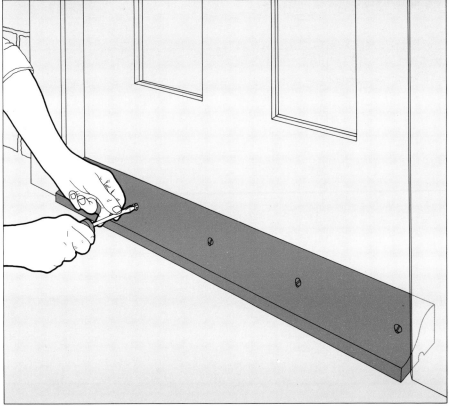

Plugging Up All the Cracks and Crannies

Houses are built of a number of different materials working together to keep out draughts, dust and moisture. Because these varied materials expand and contract at different rates with changing temperatures, cracks and gaps are bound to appear wherever two different materials meet. Traffic vibrations, the closing and opening of windows and doors, even the pressure of wind against the roof and walls, widen these openings over a period of time. If you added together these unintentional gaps in an average house—round the windows and doors, at the spots where pipes and cables enter the house, and in a surprising variety of other places *(opposite page, above)*—the total space would be equivalent to a hole roughly one-fifth of a square metre in area.

You can choose among dozens of different sealant materials to fill these gaps. All of them are airtight and watertight. Almost all come in at least two consistencies: gun grade, sold in cartridges for use with a caulking gun *(page 18)*, and suitable for cracks no wider than a pencil; and knife grade, applied to wider cracks with a putty knife. For very thin cracks, you may prefer a sealant that comes in a handy tube; for very wide ones, such as the gaps which sometimes develop round window frames, you may want to use cord or rope sealant, which comes in rolls and is easily pressed in with the fingers. Whatever sealant you use should be applied to clean, dry surfaces on a warm, dry day.

Far more important than these comparatively minor differences of consistency or packaging, however, is the chemical composition of the sealant you choose. Depending on its composition, every sealant can be assigned to one of three performance groups, shown in the chart below.

At the lowest level, in the basic group, are ropes, cords and sealants that are based on natural oils and resins. The intermediate group, which consists mainly of natural or synthetic rubbers, sticks better to most building materials and is also elastic enough to accommodate small changes in the width or depth of a crack. More modern synthetic materials make up the high-performance group; they are the most expensive of the three, but in many cases they are well worth the extra cost. These are the most versatile of all sealants, being the easiest to apply as well as the most durable—in some cases, so durable and so new that the working life of the sealant has yet to be determined.

A Sealant for Every Surface

	Special uses	Sealant	Durability (years)	Adhesion	Shrinkage resistance
Basic performance	glazing	oil and resin sealants	1 to 5	fair to good	poor
	very wide gaps	polybutane cord or rope	1 to 2	none	excellent
Intermediate performance	indoor and protected surfaces	non-acrylic latex; PVA	2 to 7	good, except to metal	fair
	indoor and protected surfaces	acrylic latex	2 to 7	excellent, except to metal	fair
	metal-to-masonry	butyl rubber	5 to 7	excellent	fair
	concrete	neoprene	10 to 15	excellent	good
High performance	anywhere	polysulphide	20	excellent	excellent
	anywhere	polyurethane	more than 20	excellent	excellent
	anywhere	silicone	more than 20	good, excellent with primer	excellent

Finding gaps and cracks. The house on the left is marked in colour at the points where sealant is generally needed. One trouble spot is not shown in the drawing: the point at which a pipe or a cable enters a room from beneath the floorboards or from an unheated attic or basement. Always seal this entry point.

Judging a sealant. All the sealants in this chart are general-purpose varieties for wood, masonry, metal and glass, but many have areas of special usefulness, listed in the first column. Use the other colums to match a specific sealant to your needs. Manufacturers' trade names rarely indicate the composition of a sealant or a cleaner to use at the end of a job—read the fine print on the label to find the generic names shown here.

Adhesion is a measure of a sealant's ability to bond to a surface; shrinkage resistance measures its ability to stay there under changing conditions. A sealant is tack-free when it loses its initial stickiness; in the curing stage, it hardens and dries to its final form. For sealants that need primers, follow the manufacturers' instructions.

Tack-free (hours)	Cure (days)	Cleaner	Primer	Paint	Comments
2 to 24	up to 1 year	paint thinner	none needed	must be painted	lowest cost; may stain surface
remains soft and pliable		no cleaning required	none needed	should not be painted	often used as temporary or seasonal sealants
¼ to 1	3	water	none needed	optional	deteriorates in sunlight; paint outdoor sealants
¼ to 1	3	water	sometimes needed on porous surfaces—follow manufacturer's instructions	optional	easy to apply in cool weather and on relatively damp surfaces
½ to 1½	7	white spirit, paint thinner	none needed	optional	good moisture resistance; relatively difficult to make into a neat bead
1	30 to 60	toluene, xylene, MEK	none needed	optional	toxic; apply only when ample ventilation can be provided
24 to 72	up to 90	toluene, TCE, MEK	primer sometimes needed—follow manufacturer's instructions	optional	non-toxic when cured, but may irritate skin when being applied
½ to 24	4 to 14	MEK, paint thinner, xylene	follow manufacturer's instructions	optional	relatively easy to apply; non-toxic when cured
¼ to 1	2 to 5	paint thinner, xylene, MEK, toluene	follow manufacturer's instructions	cannot be painted	high moisture resistance; can be applied at low temperatures; non-toxic when cured

Five Ways to Seal Cracks

Most of the newer and more efficient sealants are usually applied with a caulking gun. The most popular type uses individual cartridges *(right)* that are thrown away when empty. Getting a smooth flow of the sealant—a proper bead—may require practice. So if you are doing the job for the first time, make a few trial strokes.

While a caulking gun is best for most jobs, some small repairs are more conveniently done in other ways *(opposite page)*: sealants that are squeezed from a collapsible tube, glazing compound that is pressed into cracks with your fingers, rope-like strands that are pushed into place and filler that must be tamped into openings.

Whatever you use, thoroughly clean the area round a crack, removing old sealant and chipped paint with a wood chisel or putty knife. Wipe the crack with turpentine, then use a stiff brush to get rid of any remaining dirt. Do not try to seal when temperatures are below 10°C—the sealant will be too hard to handle easily and it will not stick to the cold surfaces.

Using a caulking gun. Hold the gun at a 45 degree angle to the surface and squeeze the trigger with a steady pressure. Keep the gun slightly slanted in the direction you are moving and draw it along slowly so that the sealant not only fills the crack but also overlaps the edges.

To get a smooth bead, fill a single seam in one stroke if you can. Pressure inside the cartridge will keep pushing out the sealant after you release the trigger; to avoid getting a lumpy bead when several strokes are necessary, release the trigger quickly at the end of each stroke and continue to move the gun as you slowly squeeze the trigger for the next stroke. When you want to stop the flow of sealant altogether, disengage the trigger by turning the plunger so that the teeth point upwards and then pull the rod backwards a couple of centimetres.

The Versatile Caulking Gun

Sealant manufacturers package their products in standard cartridges that fit interchangeably into a caulking gun. The gun pushes sealant out of the cartridge with a trigger-activated plunger. Follow the manufacturer's instructions to load a caulking gun with a cartridge.

On the model shown below, the plunger rod is turned and pulled back as far as possible, the cartridge is inserted and then the plunger rod is turned so that its teeth face down and engage the trigger mechanism. After loading the cartridge, snip off the sealed tip of its nozzle at a 45 degree angle. The nozzle is tapered so that you can make an opening for a thin, medium or heavy bead. Next, insert a nail through the tip to puncture the seal at the base of the nozzle. After use, plug the nozzle with the nail.

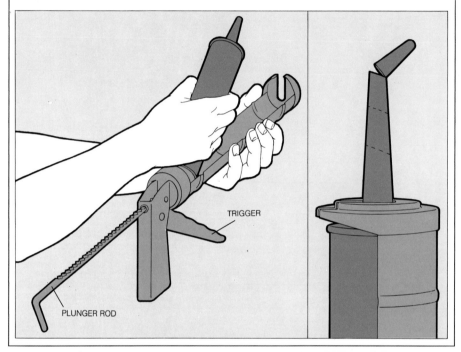

TRIGGER

PLUNGER ROD

Using a roll-up tube. For sealing round outside taps *(below)*, vents and other small areas, use a squeeze tube. Snip the tip off the nozzle in the same way as for a gun cartridge *(opposite page)* to give a bead of the desired size. Apply the sealant by squeezing the tube from the bottom—much as you would a toothpaste tube—and draw it slowly across the crack.

Sealing with glazing compound. To keep cold air from leaking round the joint between glass windowpanes and their frames, press this soft, sticky material along the edge of the glass with your fingers. Then smooth it with a putty knife. Turpentine can be used with the knife in order to make a smoother finish and it can also be used with a rag to clean off excess compound.

Applying rope-like sealant. This material, especially useful for temporary seals and hard-to-reach corners, can be purchased in different widths, depending on the size of the crack. Press it in with your fingers—wetting them will make them less likely to stick to the sealant.

Sealing large cracks. For a crack that is more than 10 mm deep—common at the joint between window or door frames and the surrounding brickwork *(above)*—first plug the crack with a foam draught-excluding material. Push the filler into the crack with a screwdriver or a putty knife. Then apply one or more beads of sealant with a caulking gun.

The Battle against Moisture

A downpipe shoe. After flowing along gutters, rainwater is channelled by downpipes to ground level. A downpipe should always be positioned above a drain, since rainwater that is discharged directly on to the soil around a house can lead to dampness in the outer wall and even structural damage resulting from soil movement. As a further safeguard, a downpipe can be fitted with an adjustable shoe *(left)*, which will ensure that the water flows into the drain without splashing the adjoining brickwork.

Damp is a danger you should never ignore. If not controlled at an early stage, it can ruin your decorations and furniture, cause serious structural damage to your house and even affect your health. Carry out an attic-to-basement inspection at least once a year; if you find evidence of damp, trace its cause and correct the problem immediately.

The three most common causes of damp are: water penetrating from the outside; moisture rising up from the ground; and water vapour condensing out of the atmosphere. Air always contains a certain amount of water vapour, and the higher the temperature, the more vapour the air can hold. However, as soon as the air cools down—for example, by coming into contact with a cold, poorly ventilated wall—some of the vapour may condense out as droplets of water.

Many condensation problems can be reduced with improved ventilation. By installing strategically placed openings in the attic and basement *(pages 60–61 and 65)*, you can ensure a continuous exchange between the warm, moist air inside the house and the drier air outside. In problem areas such as kitchens, bathrooms and laundry rooms, where the moisture content of the air is particularly high, extractor fans and ducting may provide the answer *(pages 62–64 and 66–67)*.

Penetrating damp occurs when water works its way through an exterior wall or roof. It is mainly a problem in older houses built without cavity walls—two leaves of brickwork separated by an air space—and often it is due to some simple fault, such as a blocked gutter or a broken downpipe. If you are unable to find any obvious defect, and the damp appears to be general rather than local, then you may need to improve the weather resistance of the external wall. This can be done through cladding, repointing or rendering *(pages 38–43)*. Another alternative is to apply a silicone water repellent *(page 38)*.

A frequent cause of rising damp is the absence, or breaking down, of the damp-proof course (often simply referred to as the DPC). This is a layer of impermeable material, such as slate or bituminous felt, that is inserted into the walls of a house just above ground level. Where the DPC is absent or faulty, moisture rises up the walls from the soil and is absorbed by the brickwork.

Unfortunately, it is not always easy to distinguish between the various kinds of damp. For example, one form of penetrating damp located at the foot of an inside wall and often mistaken for rising damp is caused by "backsplash"—water issuing from a downpipe and splashing back on to the wall instead of away from it *(opposite)*. Dampness may also have more than one source—a wall that becomes saturated through rising damp, for example, is quite likely to be affected by condensation as well. Some of the more common causes of damp in a house are described overleaf. However, where you are unable to identify the cause yourself, you would be well advised to consult a damp-proofing specialist or a qualified surveyor.

Detecting the Causes of Damp

To protect your house from the ruinous effects of damp, you should carry out regular and systematic inspections, paying particular attention to the danger areas listed below. When you discover a problem, take steps to correct it as soon as possible to minimize the damage.

Loose, broken or missing roof tiles or slates are the most common cause of roof leaks. Fortunately, faults are easy to detect and simple to repair *(pages 24–29)*. Flaws in the flashing—the strips of material, usually metal, that form a junction between the chimney stack and the roof, and between one section of roof and another—should be repaired as soon as they show signs of deterioration *(pages 32–33)*.

When a flue is disused, check that the chimney pots have been removed or properly capped, to prevent damp from soaking down to the chimney breast below. The chimney stack and the flaunching—the layer of mortar which holds the chimney pots in place—should also be maintained in good repair.

During and after heavy rain, irregular but well-defined patches of penetrating damp may appear on the inside of exterior walls. Although they may leave an efflorescent stain, these patches tend to disappear in dry weather. Serious problems can occur when a gutter or downpipe becomes blocked or broken. Rainwater will pour directly on to the wall, wearing away mortar joints and seeping through brickwork. Gutters and downpipes need regular maintenance—painting, patching, repositioning—and replacement when they wear out *(pages 34–37)*.

Another site for damp penetration is around door and window frames; where gaps have appeared due to shrinkage or weathering, they should be sealed with a sealant *(page 18)*. Check the drip channels on the underside of window sills; if they are blocked or damaged, rain water can run along the underside of the sill and into the brickwork.

Generally, rendering an external wall provides good protection against penetration by moisture. However, rendering that is in poor condition may crack and pull away from the wall, enabling water to seep behind the rendering and soak the brickwork. If the weather is very cold, the water may freeze in the cracks, forcing out large chunks of rendering and making the wall even more vulnerable to damp penetration. The solution to the problem is either to apply new rendering or to cover the wall with cladding *(pages 38–43)*.

Although the solid walls of older houses are particularly prone to penetrating damp, the cavity walls of modern houses are by no means immune. If mortar has fallen on to the ties that span the cavity, damp is able to cross from the outer to the inner leaf. However, several sections of brickwork need to be removed in order to reach the ties, so it is best to leave this task to a professional builder.

Serious damage can also be caused by rising damp, the result of moisture in the ground rising up the walls of the house by capillary action. The most obvious sign of rising damp is a continuous tide-mark that can extend for as much as 1 metre above the skirting board. Unlike penetrating damp, rising damp does not depend on the weather, though heavy rain may intensify the problem. The effects can range from discoloured wallpaper to widespread destruction of plaster and woodwork. Fungal decay may also take hold in door frames, floorboards and skirtings.

Rising damp usually occurs where there is no DPC (damp-proof course), or where the DPC has deteriorated or is badly positioned *(pages 44–47)*. But it can also occur if the DPC is bridged—for example, by sand being heaped against an outside wall. The earth level should be at least 150 mm below the DPC; if it is not, then lower the ground level.

A damp cellar or basement may be caused by an inadequate drainage system that is unable to channel excess water away from foundation walls. Where damp works its way through a solid concrete floor, this is usually due to the absence of, or a fault in, the damp-proof membrane—the layer of impermeable material that stretches under the floor and up the walls to overlap the DPC *(page 55)*.

Checking for faults. Carry out an inspection of the whole house, both inside and out, at least once a year, starting with the roof and working systematically down to the basement. Make a careful note of any faults that may allow damp to enter the house *(right)*, and carry out the necessary repair work as a matter of priority.

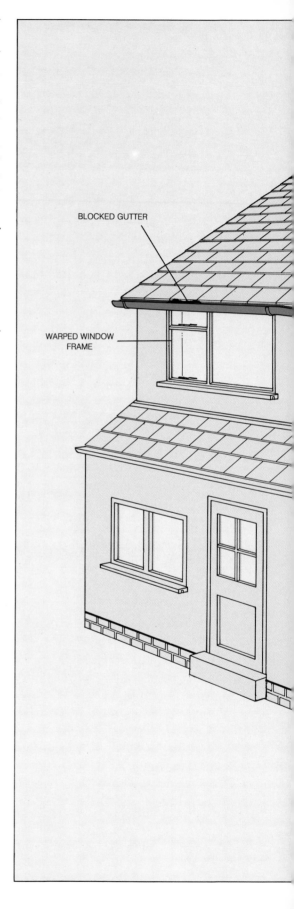

BLOCKED GUTTER

WARPED WINDOW FRAME

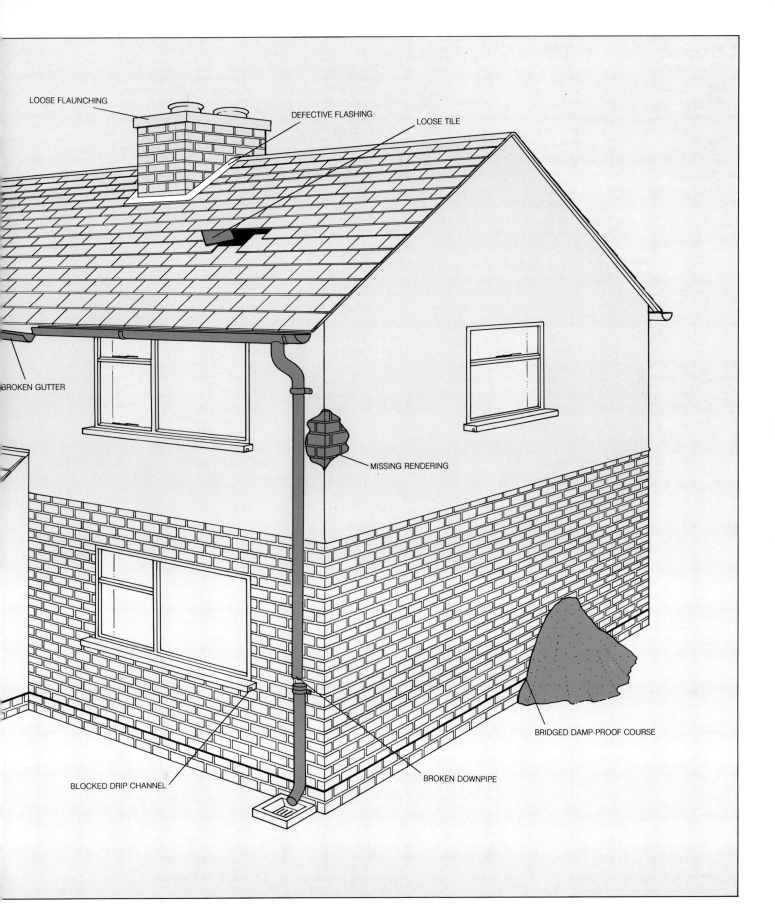

LOOSE FLAUNCHING

DEFECTIVE FLASHING

LOOSE TILE

BROKEN GUTTER

MISSING RENDERING

BRIDGED DAMP-PROOF COURSE

BLOCKED DRIP CHANNEL

BROKEN DOWNPIPE

Roof Leaks: Hard to Find, Easy to Fix

The old joke that a roof leaks only during a downpour, when you can't fix it, is at least half wrong—the trickiest part of repairing a leak is finding it, and that may be easier when the water is coming through. Even then, do not assume that the damage is near the drip, for the multi-layered construction of modern roofs *(below)* can lead water on a long and twisting course over several layers and through a variety of joints before it finally pours into the house. Often, the water will travel down inside a first-storey wall and across a ground-floor ceiling before finally gushing out around a lighting fixture.

Some leaks are caused by dislodged or damaged tiles, which you may be able to see from outside the house. But equally common—and far less easy to spot—are small openings in the strips of flashing that should be installed around vents and chimneys and at corners. The inevitable expansion and contraction of house mate-rials loosen the roofing cement that holds the edges of flashing in position. The cement may also crumble with age, and it should be checked and renewed if necessary every few years.

Although a leak that must be sealed may be far from the visible drip of water, start your exploration there. Look for damage to the roof in the general area overhead. Alternatively, try to trace the leak from interior evidence—even slight discoloration in a wall or ceiling covering suggests the presence of moisture.

On the roof itself, always take on jobs of preventive maintenance as well as patch-ing existing leaks. Check the flashings and reseal them if necessary *(pages 32–33)*—the same technique will work for leaks in a roof made entirely of metal—and replace missing or damaged tiles.

Traditionally, roof tiles were made of clay, but many modern tiles are made of concrete, which is slightly cheaper as well as more durable. Tiles are divided into two basic types: plain (or double lap) and single lap. In the case of plain tiles, each row overlaps the one below, which means that there are at least two thicknesses of tile in every part of the roof.

However, in the case of single-lap tiles, the overlap is minimal, so that the roof is covered by only a single thickness of tile. There are also other differences. Plain tiles butt together at the sides and the vertical joins in each row are staggered. But single-lap tiles interlock at the sides and the vertical joins are aligned.

Whether you need to replace plain or single-lap tiles, the procedure is much the same. The main differences are in the spac-ing of the battens to which the tiles are fixed and the number of nails—if any—that are needed. Always lay new tiles in the same way as the old ones were fixed originally—and match replacement tiles to the existing ones.

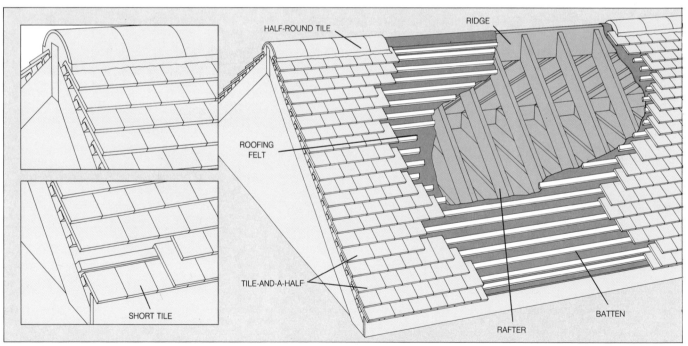

The anatomy of a roof. Most house roofs are pitched at an angle on both sides of a central ridge. Rafters are laid from the walls to the ridge, and the roof covering—plain tiles, single-lap tiles or slates *(pages 28–29)*—is fixed to timber battens nailed at right angles to the rafters. To improve insulation, rolls of bitumin-ous roofing felt are laid horizontally beneath the battens and over the rafters. These are then fixed to the rafters with either nails or staples. Where the roof is covered with single-lap tiles or slates, each course must be nailed to a batten. However, where plain tiles are used *(above)*, it is usually sufficient for every fourth or fifth course to be nailed. This is because most plain tiles have two small protrusions, or nibs, on the underside which allow them to be hooked over the battens. Single-lap tiles are available in a variety of shapes and sizes, but plain tiles are usually 265 by 165 mm, and 13 mm thick. In addition to a standard tile for the main roof area, there are also tiles specially designed for other parts of the roof: a tile—called a tile-and-a-half—half as wide again as the standard size is used at the end of alternate courses; a short tile is used along the eaves and the ridge; and a half-round tile is used to cap the ridge itself.

Repairing a Tiled Roof

1 Removing damaged tiles. Wedge small pieces of timber under the tiles immediately above the one to be replaced. If the damaged tile is nibbed, lever it upwards with a bricklayer's trowel to disengage the nibs from the batten. You can then use the trowel to ease it away from the surrounding tiles. If a tile is nailed, you may be able to work it loose through a combination of rocking and levering. If this fails, use a slate ripper *(pages 28–29)* to cut away the heads of the nails. Work from the eaves upwards when removing tiles from more than one course.

WEDGES

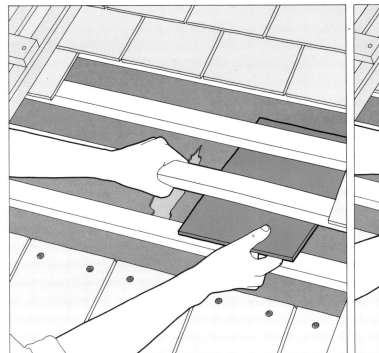

2 Replacing torn felt. If you find that the roofing felt underneath damaged tiles is also faulty, fit a new piece. Begin the repair by removing the nails that hold the exposed sections of batten to the rafters. Then slide a hardboard offcut, smooth side down, under the battens near the tear. Move the hardboard along until it rests on a rafter at one side of the tear.

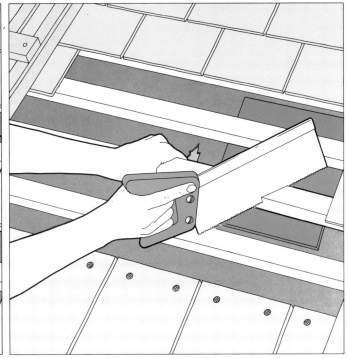

3 Cutting the battens. Angle-cut the battens with a small saw, using the hardboard to protect the felt from further damage *(above)*. Reposition the hardboard over the rafter on the other side of the tear and cut through the battens in the same way. If the felt is sound but the battens are damaged, you should still follow the procedures described here and in Steps 5 and 6 *(overleaf)*.

4 Cutting away the felt. With a sharp utility knife, cut a square, slightly larger than the damaged area, out of the roofing felt. Cut a new piece of felt slightly larger than the square removed, making sure you leave a big enough margin for gluing. Spread bitumen adhesive around the edges of the felt patch and press it firmly over the hole. You can buy an offcut of roofing felt from a builders' merchant.

5 Measuring up for new battens. Battens used for hanging tiles vary in size, so use the old battens as a guide to the dimensions required. Measure the distance between the cut ends of the old battens and cut new pieces to fit the gap.

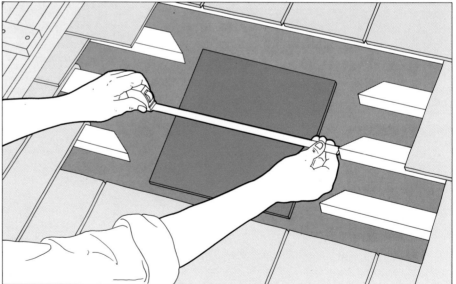

6 **Fixing new battens.** Brush the new pieces of batten with a wood preservative and nail them in place on the rafters using galvanized or sherardized nails. At the same time, nail down the loose ends of the old battens.

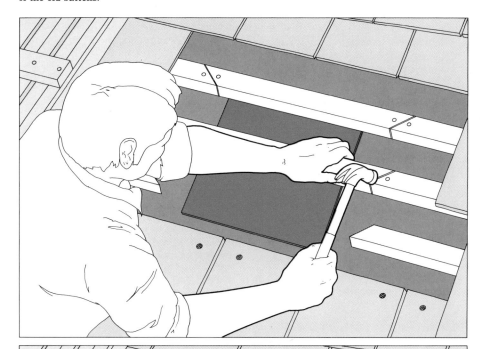

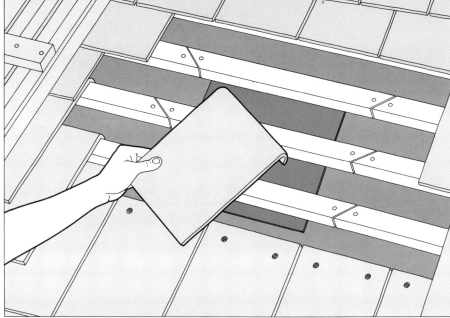

7 **Hanging new tiles.** Hang the new tiles in the order in which you removed the old ones, working from the eaves upwards. Hook the nibbed tiles over the battens and nail them in place only if the original tiles were nailed. Always nail tiles without nibs. When all the tiles have been hung, sweep debris from the repair areas and gutters.

Some Do's and Dont's for Roofing Work

Working on a pitched roof is potentially dangerous: if you fear heights, or if your roof is steeply pitched, the job is best left to a professional. But you can make repairs safely by taking the following common-sense precautions:

☐ Never work in wet, cold or windy weather. Roofing materials can become dangerously slippery when wet.

☐ Wear shoes that have slip-resistant soles, and choose loose-fitting clothes so that you can move about freely.

☐ Use an access ladder that extends well above the eaves so you need never step over the top of the ladder. The ladder should be tied securely to a hook screwed into the fascia board or an exposed rafter end. If the gutters are made of plastic, the top of the ladder must be held clear of them with a ladder stay.

☐ Keep your hips between the rails as you climb, and never lean over the side of the ladder to work.

☐ Enlist a helper to steady the ladder as you climb and to pass up tools and materials once you are at the top.

☐ When working on a steep roof, use a roof ladder or crawling board with timber or metal brackets that hook over the roof ridge *(below)*. These ladders not only provide secure hand and footholds, but distribute your weight evenly as you climb to protect brittle roofing materials such as tiles and slates.

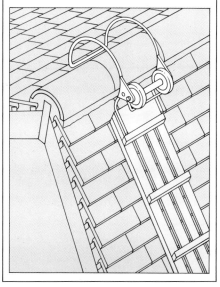

Tackling Repairs to Slate Roofs

Slate is not only one of the most attractive roofing materials but, when properly installed and maintained, it is also one of the most durable—a slate roof should last for at least 50 years. It is constructed in the same way as a plain tiled roof *(page 24)*: slates are laid from the eaves upwards in overlapping courses, with the vertical joins between slates staggered in adjacent rows. Thus, any one slate partly covers the two slates below it.

Slates usually become loose either because they have cracked or because the nails that hold them in place have rusted. If the problem is due to rust, you can be fairly sure that the installer failed to use corrosion-resistant nails, in which case it is probably best to have the whole roof refixed by a competent professional.

Cracks or breaks are most likely to occur in relatively porous, moisture-absorbing slates; when the temperature falls below freezing, the water expands and cracks the slate. When cracks do appear, act quickly.

Work from a crawling board securely anchored at the ridge with roof hooks like those shown on page 27. You can seal hairline cracks with bituminous mastic or make a temporary repair *(below)*, but any badly cracked or broken slates must be replaced with new ones.

Like single-lap tiles, slates are always nailed to the roofing battens. They may be either head nailed—fixed at the top—or centre nailed—fixed about half way down. Use a slate ripper or hacksaw blade to cut through the heads of old nails.

Since slates vary in size, shape and thickness, take a damaged one along as a guide when buying replacements. If you are unable to find an exact match, buy the next largest size of the same thickness and cut the slates to fit *(Step 2, opposite page)*.

New slates can be obtained from builders' merchants, either singly or in bulk. If you decide to buy second-hand slates—which is usually more economical—make sure they are undamaged.

A quick fix with a metal patch. To repair a badly damaged slate temporarily, make a patch from a sheet of copper or aluminium flashing. With a pair of metal shears, cut the patch to twice the width and about 75 mm longer than the slate. Apply roofing cement to the centre of the patch, then slide the patch up under the slate, cemented side down. Continue pushing the patch upwards, using a wood block and hammer to tap it if necessary, until its top edge passes the bottom edge of the slates in the next course.

METAL PATCH

Replacing Broken Slates

1 **Removing the damaged slate.** Slide the end of a slate ripper under the damaged slate and hook one of the two sharp ripper notches around a nail holding the slate in place. With a hammer, strike sharply down against the ripper handle to cut through the nail; repeat on the other nail and pull the damaged slate free. If you have no slate ripper, use a hacksaw blade.

2 **Cutting a new slate to size.** Using the damaged slate as a guide, mark both sides of the replacement. Score along the lines on each side repeatedly with a cold chisel. Set a scored line at the edge of a flat surface and snap off the excess. Smooth the edges with emery cloth.

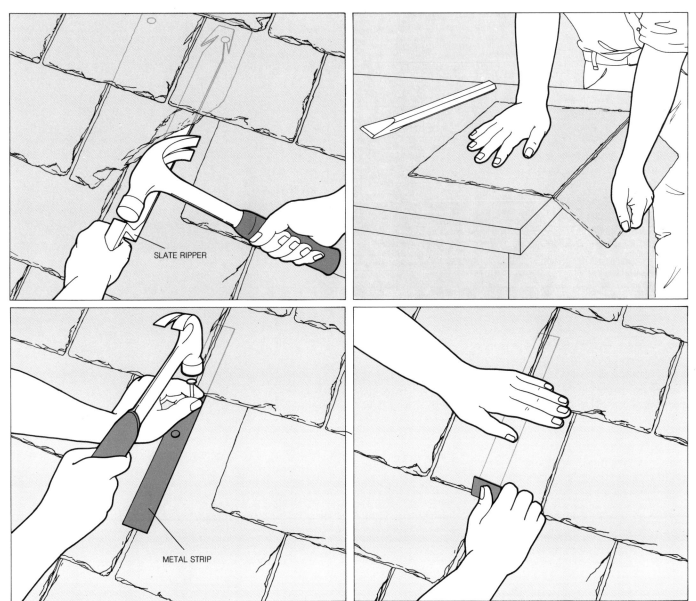

SLATE RIPPER

METAL STRIP

3 **Installing a tingle.** To hold the new slate in place, cut a tingle—a strip of metal flashing 25 mm wide and long enough to run for several millimetres under the slates in the course above and about 50 mm below the bottom edge of the replacement slate. Using nails of the same metal, fasten the tingle to the batten between the two underlying slates.

4 **Securing the new slate.** Slide the new slate over the tingle and push it upwards under the slates in the course above. When it is correctly aligned with the slates on either side, bend the tingle up around its bottom edge to fix it in position.

Repairing Flat Roofs

Roofs that are flat or nearly flat are usually built up with three layers of roofing felt bonded together over a base of wooden boarding. The first layer of overlapped felt sheets is nailed to the boarding. Each of the two subsequent layers is bonded to the one beneath using either bitumastic (also known as cold mastic), which is applied cold and is useful for small repairs, or a bitumen-based solid compound, such as asphalt, which has to be liquefied by heating before it can be applied.

This built-up roofing is often topped with a protective covering of gravel, pebbles or marble chips, which help reflect the sun's rays from the dark, heat-absorbent surface of the felt.

A built-up roof should last from 10 to 20 years, before the sun's heat dries out the bonding material and cracks develop over the entire surface. When the roof does eventually fail, do not try to replace it yourself—that job calls for special equipment and the expertise of a professional roofer. But you can and should repair minor damage as it occurs. Inspect the roof at least once a year for blisters, cracks and tears. Blisters, which indicate that roofing felt has separated from the underlying layers or from the wooden boarding, should be treated immediately by the method shown on the right, before they break open and admit rainwater.

As you treat a blister, examine its interior. If it is dry, the blister is probably caused by poorly adhering or dried-out bonding material, and a simple patch can be an adequate repair. Interior moisture is a sign that water has leaked into the roofing and seeped along the boarding to a point underneath the blister. Locate the point of leakage. If a substantial amount of water has penetrated the roofing, causing a large section to buckle or blister, cut out and patch the entire area *(opposite page)*.

Treating a Blister

1 Cutting the blister open. Use a stiff brush to sweep dirt and loose gravel or mineral granules away from the blistered area. Then slice the blister open lengthwise with a hook-nosed linoleum knife *(right)* or a utility knife. If the felt layers beneath the surface are dry, proceed directly to Step 2. If they are damp, deepen the cut down to the wooden boarding and let the roofing dry out (you can use a hair drier to speed the process) before proceeding to Step 2. To locate the source of the leak, feel for the spongy lines or patches leading from the blister to a faulty flashing or other damaged area. Repair that area as shown opposite.

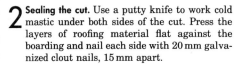

2 Sealing the cut. Use a putty knife to work cold mastic under both sides of the cut. Press the layers of roofing material flat against the boarding and nail each side with 20 mm galvanized clout nails, 15 mm apart.

3 Patching the cut. Cut a patch of roofing felt large enough to overlap the blistered area about 50 mm in every direction. Cover an equivalent area over the cut with cold mastic and press the patch into place. Fasten the new patch at its edges with 20 mm clout nails, and then cover the nail heads and the edges of the patch with additional cold mastic.

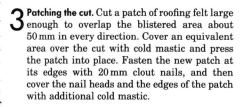

Putting In a Patch

1 **Removing the damaged section.** Begin the repair of a large tear or a large blistered or buckled area by scraping away any surrounding gravel; then cut out a square or rectangle that includes the damage. Dip your knife in turpentine as you work to keep the blade free of tar and felt fibres, and pull out the layers of felt individually. If water has soaked the felt, remove all the roofing within the rectangle down to the boarding, and let the area dry thoroughly.

2 **Rebuilding the roofing.** Using one of the damaged layers as a guide, cut matching patches from new roofing felt—one patch for each layer you have removed. Coat the bottom of the exposed roofing with cold mastic, and work additional mastic under the edges of the adjoining material. Lay a felt patch in the mastic bed, press it into place, and coat its top with more cold mastic. Continue rebuilding the roofing layer by layer with patches until it is level with the surrounding area. Nail the top patch down with 20 mm clout nails spaced evenly around the edges.

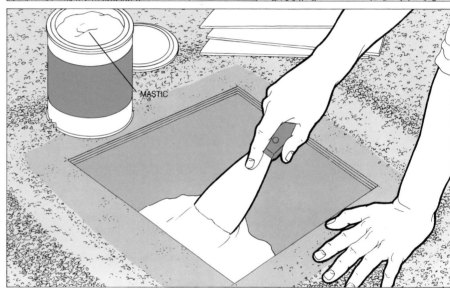

3 **Adding a protective covering.** If the original roofing was covered with a layer of mineral-surfaced roll roofing, cut an oversized patch of the same material and press it into a bed of cold mastic over the patched area. Nail down the edges of the patch, then cover the nail heads and patch the edges with mastic. If the finish consists of gravel or marble chips, spread a thick layer of mastic over the top patch of roofing felt, sprinkle gravel or chips over the mastic, and press the stones firmly into the mastic with a flat board.

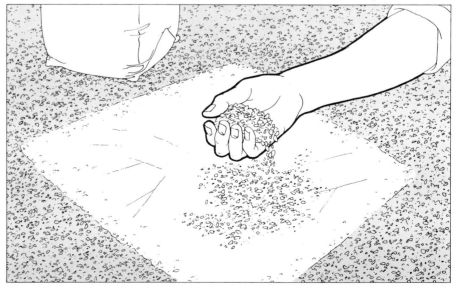

Flashing for the Weak Points

The weakest points in a roof, from a weather-proofing viewpoint, are the angles where slopes meet to form a valley and where chimneys and vent pipes project through the roofing. To protect these vulnerable areas of the roof, flashing is installed to make watertight seals between adjoining structures or surfaces. But without regular inspection and preventive maintenance, any flashing can become a funnel directing water into your house instead of into the gutters and downpipes.

Some roofers prefer to use flashings made up from double layers of bituminous roofing felt. More expensive, but also more effective, are flashings of rust-resistant metals such as lead, zinc, copper or aluminium. Self-adhesive flashing strips, usually consisting of heavy-duty aluminium foil with a bitumen adhesive backing, are also available. Some older houses have flashings of galvanized steel.

The life of more rust-prone flashings can be considerably extended if rust spots are removed promptly with a wire brush and the flashings are painted periodically with metal primer and aluminium paint.

Metal flashings should also be protected against galvanic corrosion. This is caused by an electrochemical reaction that occurs where dissimilar types of metal come into prolonged contact. It is important, therefore, when repairing or replacing flashings, to make sure that the new metal and nails you use are the same material as the existing ones.

Roof valleys take some of the hardest wear because they channel water from two adjacent roof slopes into the gutter. Cracks or holes in the valley flashing can be repaired with a metal patch *(right)*. But if the damage is extensive, the whole run of flashing will have to be replaced. This is a major job that involves removing the tiles or slates at either side of the valley, and you may prefer to leave it to a professional.

Chimney flashing is more complex—and more vulnerable to leaks—than other roof flashings. In the best installations, flashings are fitted to both the chimney stack and the surrounding roof area *(opposite page, top)*. This construction allows slight movement and settlement without damage to the waterproof seal. However, the flashings for chimneys often consist of no more than single pieces of metal attached to the sides of the stack. The methods of repair are similar for both types.

The most common problem with chimney flashings is deterioration of mortar or other seals; water then runs behind the top edge of the flashing and down the chimney into the house. Loose mortar should be replaced and all flashing joints resealed with bituminous mastic *(opposite page, bottom)*.

Loose or worn flashing round a vent pipe is also serious, but you can now obtain pre-sized metal and plastic pipe flashing, so replacement is more practical than repair.

Repairing valley flashing. If you discover water-marks or other signs of damage inside the attic under the valley of a roof, inspect the flashing for cracks or holes. To repair a metal flashing, first clean round the damaged area thoroughly with a wire brush. Then apply a thin coating of bituminous mastic with a putty knife *(above)*, lay a patch of matching metal over the top and press down. Make sure that the metal patch overlaps the damaged area of the flashing by about 6 mm all round. Once the metal patch is firmly bedded, apply further mastic to seal the edges. Use felt patches to seal tears in flashing made of roofing felt, following the instructions for repairing flat roofs *(pages 30–31)*.

To ensure that no small cracks have been missed, cover the entire flashing with two or three coats of bituminous waterproofer. This is available in several finishes, including white, brick red, ivy green and slate grey.

Resealing a Chimney

The design of a watertight chimney seal depends on whether the chimney is sited on or below the roof ridge. If it is sited below the ridge (right), the seal should be made up of three main components—a gutter flashing at the back, flashing at the sides and an apron flashing at the front. If the chimney is sited on the ridge, the gutter flashing can be dispensed with. Instead, two front aprons should be installed—one on either side of the ridge.

Angled into the junction between the stack and the roof, the apron should overlap each by at least 150 mm. The lip of the apron is slotted into a raked out mortar joint and wedged in place with wooden wedges or plugs of the same metal. The joint is then repointed. A back gutter should form a 100 mm overlap with the stack and a 225 mm overlap with the roof; unlike the apron, it is held in place at one end by the roof covering.

The side flashings consist of two parts—L-shaped base flashings, or soakers, which are laid between the tiles adjoining the stack, and stepped cover flashings, which are tucked into the mortar joints of the stack and protect the tops of the soakers.

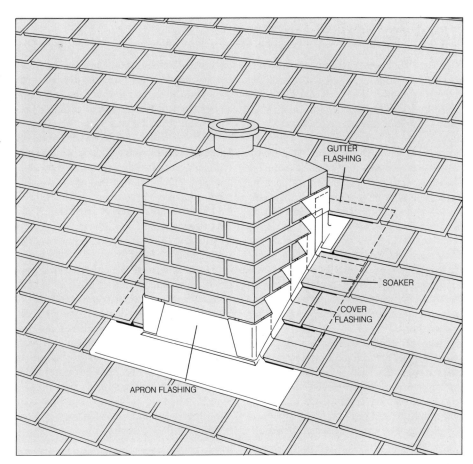

1 **Cleaning the mortar joint.** Prise the loose cover flashings out of the mortar joint and lay them aside. Using a cold chisel and hammer, remove 20 mm of mortar from the joint (above). Check that the top edge of the exposed soakers are flush with the brickwork and seal the edge with mastic as necessary.

2 **Installing the flashing.** Dampen the open joint with a wet brush and insert the lip of the cover flashing in the joint. Using a tool called a joint filler, slide mortar off the edge of a board and tamp it into the joint, filling the space (above). When the mortar is firm but not hard, finish by shaping it to match the other joints.

3 **Sealing the joints.** Inspect the rest of the chimney for any crumbling mortar joints and repair them following Steps 1 and 2. Then seal all of the joints with a liberal coating of non-hardening mastic, making sure that it overlaps them by about 50 mm on either side.

How to Make Gutters Work

If gutters or downpipes become blocked, rainwater will pour off the eaves, soaking the outside walls and eventually seeping into the house. So it is important to keep your guttering in good repair. Inspect it at least once a year, sweeping out the accumulated debris with a hand brush and trowel. Flush out the gutter with water; it should flow steadily towards the downpipe outlet. If it overflows the outlet, this means that the downpipe is blocked and needs to be cleared (below, left).

To ensure a good flow of water to the downpipe, gutters are fixed on a slight incline. However, a bent bracket or loose fixing screw often causes a gutter to sag, so that the flow of water is impeded. In this case, it is necessary to realign the gutter (below, right).

Although plastic is now the most common material for rainwater systems, many older properties still have gutters and downpipes made of cast iron. Provided regular maintenance is carried out, and rust is not allowed to take hold, iron guttering will continue to provide efficient drainage.

Use a stiff wire brush to remove small patches of rust, and treat the surface with a rust inhibitor. You should then apply one or two coats of rust-resistant primer or bitumen paint to form a strong protective layer. If you wish to paint over the bitumen paint, however, you will have to cover it with an aluminium spirit-based sealer. Cracks or holes can be filled with an epoxy repair material or patched with aluminium faced self-adhesive sealing strip. If the leak is severe, or if the hole is too large to be patched, you will have to replace the affected section (opposite page). Where possible, take a piece of the old guttering to a builders' merchant so that you can be sure of obtaining a matching replacement.

Because it is very heavy, cast-iron guttering is usually only available in lengths of 1.8 metres. Like plastic guttering, each cast-iron length has a moulded collar at one end which serves as a socket for the spigot end of the adjoining length. The lengths are held together with nuts and bolts, and the joints are sealed with a non-hardening mastic compound.

If the whole system is affected, however, the best solution is to replace it with guttering made of plastic (overleaf), which is light, easy to fix and requires little or no maintenance. Plastic systems come with their own brackets and fixings, as well as with detailed installation instructions.

If the gutter stands away from the wall, it must be connected to the downpipe with a swan neck, or offset (page 37). An offset consists of a socket bend, a spigot bend and a linking section of pipe. The bends come as part of the system, but the pipe will need to be cut to length.

Both metal and plastic guttering comes in three shapes: half round, square and O.G.—a cross between half round and square. Half-round and square guttering always rests in brackets fixed to the fascia board or rafter ends. O.G. guttering can either be supported on brackets or screwed directly to the fascia board.

If you are using a ladder that extends beyond the eaves, when inspecting or working on guttering, use a ladder stay to hold the ladder away from the gutter.

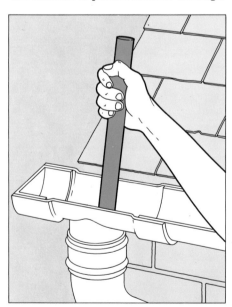

Unblocking a downpipe. Tie a rag to one end of a long pole and use this as a plunger to clear away any obstruction (above). Then flush the pipe with a hose. If the pipe is connected to the gutter by an angled section, use a length of stiff wire in place of the pole. To ensure that no debris enters the drain, place a bowl at the ground outlet.

Fitting a downpipe cage. To prevent a downpipe from clogging with leaves and debris, fit a wire cage or strainer, obtainable from most builders' merchants, into the entrance of the downpipe. Periodically inspect the gutter and clear away debris that could become matted round the cage, impeding the flow of water.

Realigning gutters. To determine whether a gutter is sagging, spray the highest point of the system with a garden hose (above). If pools of water collect in the gutter, you need to realign it, either by installing new brackets or, in the case of guttering fixed directly to the fascia, by replacing the screws. Drive a couple of strong nails into the fascia about 25 mm below the gutter to give support while it is being refitted. Plug the screw holes and refix with new, galvanized screws.

Replacing a Cast Iron Gutter

1 **Removing the damaged section.** Remove the bolts on either side of the damaged section. If these have locked solid with rust, apply a little penetrating oil to loosen them. If this fails, saw through the bolts with a hacksaw *(right)* and prise the sections apart. With O.G. guttering, first release the screws holding the section to the fascia board before undoing the section bolts.

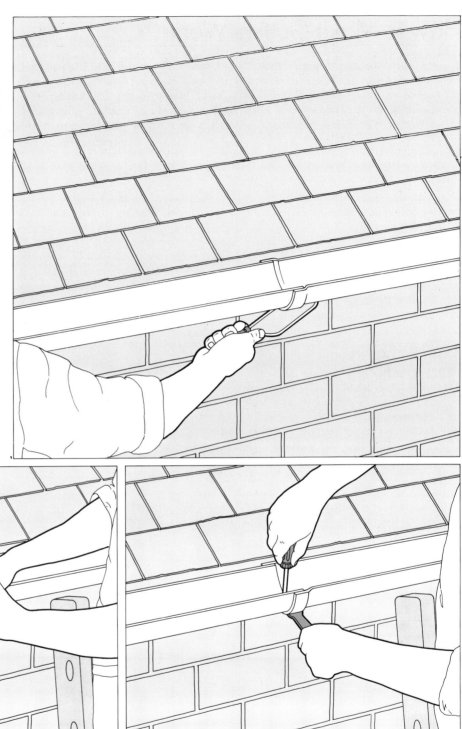

2 **Preparing the joints.** Before installing the new section, clean the remaining halves of the old joints. Scrape off all traces of sealing compound with a chisel and scour thoroughly with a stiff wire brush. Apply fresh sealing compound to the socket halves of the joints *(above)*, spreading it in an even layer about 6 mm thick.

3 **Sealing the joints.** Press the replacement section of guttering into position and insert new galvanized bolts into the ready-drilled holes of the joints. While steadying the bolt with a screwdriver, gently tighten the securing nut with a spanner so that the joint closes up and squeezes out any excess compound *(above)*. Trim away the excess with a putty knife.

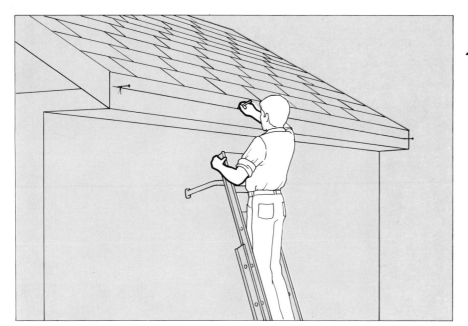

Installing a Plastic Gutter

1 **Marking the incline.** Stretch a length of string between two nails driven into the fascia board at either end of the intended gutter run. After checking with a spirit level that the line is level, lower the end near the site of the downpipe to mark the incline needed for the run. Use a ratio of at least 5 mm for every 3 metres of length. Using the line as a guide, mark the positions for the brackets at the intervals recommended by the manufacturer. Usually there are four brackets to each standard 3 metre length of guttering.

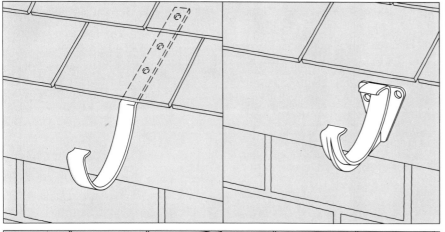

2 **Fixing the brackets.** Two types of bracket are commonly used to suspend gutters: the rafter *(far left)* and the fascia *(left)*. The rafter bracket has a long arm which is fixed to either the top of the rafter end—as shown here—or to the side. To replace a rafter bracket fixed from the top, you must first remove the roof tiles *(pages 24–27)* immediately above it. Fascia brackets are screwed directly into the fascia board. Install the end brackets first and work progressively along the chalk line, fitting the intermediate brackets.

3 **Hanging the gutter.** Starting at the higher end of the run, clip the guttering into the brackets *(left)*. When you are fitting several sections, join them together with union clips, lined with rubber seals, or gaskets, to make them watertight. A jointing cement is sometimes used instead of, or in addition to, gaskets. The method depends on the design of your system, so it is important to follow the manufacturer's instructions.

Installing a Plastic Downpipe

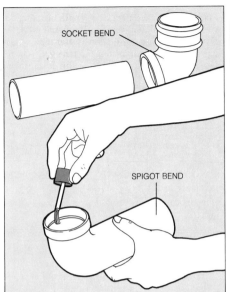

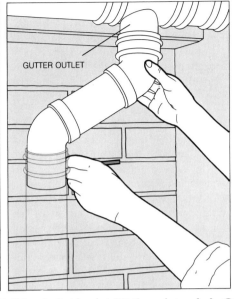

1 **Assembling an offset.** Measure the straight pipe of the old offset and cut the new one accordingly, using a fine-toothed saw. Smooth the cut edges with a fine file. Brush weld cement on to the joints of the socket and spigot bends and fit them to the pipe. Leave to dry for 5 minutes.

2 **Fixing the first bracket.** Fit the socket end of the assembled offset temporarily in place on the gutter outlet pipe and mark the wall where the other end of the offset will be connected to the downpipe. Hold the first downpipe bracket over the nearest mortar joint directly below this point and mark the screw holes. Use a power drill fitted with a 13 mm masonry bit to drill holes deep enough to take 40 mm screws. Plug the holes and screw the bracket into place.

3 **Securing the downpipe.** Hold the pipe steady against the wall so that the socket end is lined up with the bracket. Then fit a retaining clip over the socket groove, pulling the ends of the clip round the centrepiece of the bracket. When the holes in the ends of the clip are aligned with the hole in the centrepiece of the bracket, push a bolt through. Finally, fit a spring washer and tighten the nut *(above)*.

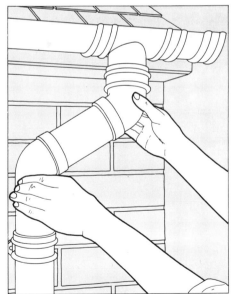

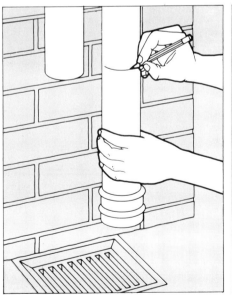

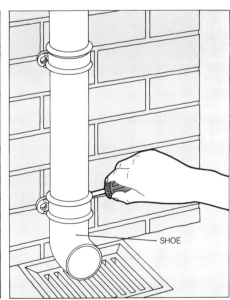

4 **Securing the offset.** Once the downpipe is in place, you can secure the offset. Vertical joints in plastic rainwater systems normally slot together without sealing. In this case, simply push the socket end of the offset on to the gutter outlet pipe, and fit the other end into the top of the downpipe *(above)*.

5 **Extending the downpipe.** The pipe should extend to just above drain level. If it does not, hold a further length of pipe, socket end down, alongside the gap and mark off as much as you need *(above)*. Saw off the required length and file the edges. Fit the socket end to the first length of pipe and secure with a bracket and clip.

6 **Attaching the shoe.** Fit the socket end of the shoe to the downpipe and again secure it to the wall with a bracket and retaining clip *(above)*. Finally, flush out the downpipe with a hose to check for leaks.

Protecting Exterior Walls against Moisture

A brick wall may look completely weatherproof, but the fact is that all building bricks are porous to some extent and will soak up wind-driven rain and other moisture. Moisture can also seep through any crumbling or poorly finished mortar joints, penetrating to the inner surface of a wall even if it is built of such weather-resistant materials as dense brick, concrete block or natural stone.

A damp wall can, of course, play havoc with internal decorations, as well as promote rotting of timber floors and other woodwork. Moreover, the heat loss from damp masonry can be up to 50 per cent greater than from dry. This affects not only solid walls, but also cavity walls filled with thermal insulating material. Indeed, insulation may actually compound the problem by transmitting moisture that would otherwise evaporate inside the cavity. So ensuring that the outside of a wall is weatherproof makes sense whatever its type of construction.

The best protection is to cover the wall completely—either with a cement-based rendering or with cladding. Although rendering *(pages 40–43)* is the more difficult of the two treatments, it is much cheaper than cladding and you should not be deterred from tackling it, particularly if you have done some internal plastering.

Rendering is applied in either two or three coats and may be given a variety of finishes, ranging from plain to pebble dash. The type of finish is largely a matter of personal choice, but the number of coats depends on the amount of grip provided by the wall surface and the rate at which it absorbs moisture—properties known respectively as key and suction.

Where these are adequate—as on rough, porous surfaces, such as clay, sandlime and thin concrete—a good bond will be formed, in which case you need apply only one undercoat and a topcoat. Where they are inadequate—as on strong, smooth surfaces, such as dense clay and stiff concrete—the bond will be poor, in which case you should apply a thin, rough-surfaced base coat.

A base coat may also be necessary for surfaces with adequate key, but excessive suction—aerated concrete and the softer types of bricks, for example. A simple way of checking for suction is to splash the wall with water. If suction is too low, the water will run off as droplets. If it is too high, the water will soak in almost immediately.

Having decided on the number of coats, you must then prepare the wall thoroughly. The whole surface should be brushed free of dust, moulds, lichens and anything else likely to prevent a satisfactory bond. Except where you are applying a three-coat treatment, mortar joints in brickwork should also be raked out.

If the task of cladding or rendering appears too daunting, you can apply an exterior wall paint instead. Of the various types available, the cheapest is cement paint, which comes in powder form to be mixed with water just before use. It provides an attractive enough finish, but forms a poor base for any subsequent coating. And although it can be applied on top of practically all undecorated surfaces, it is unsuitable for direct application to existing paintwork.

A better alternative is exterior-grade emulsion. Fast drying and easy to apply, it is resistant to both dampness and alkaline action, and gives good adhesion for subsequent coats. Bear in mind, however, that paint can only work effectively on a sound and properly prepared surface.

Where you wish to weatherproof a wall without altering its appearance, use one of the colourless sealants specially designed for masonry. Applied by brush or spray, such sealants are usually based on silicone resins, which line the pores of the wall to make it water repellent without sealing the surface. In this way, any moisture contained within the wall is able to evaporate.

If the sealant is applied according to the manufacturer's instructions, a life of 10 years may be expected from one application to surfaces of normal porosity. Exceptionally porous surfaces may need another coat. Sealants require a sound surface, so it is essential to repair cracks or defective mortar joints before applying them.

Repointing Mortar Joints

1 Chiselling out. Remove old mortar to a depth of 15 mm, using a cold chisel and club hammer. Brush out and dampen the joints. Prepare new mortar with 1 part Portland cement to 3 parts fine sand and enough water to give a rich, stiff mix.

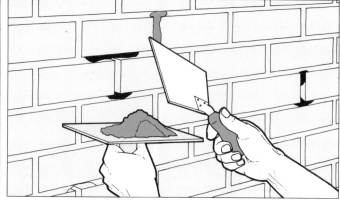

2 Laying in. Load some of the mortar on to a hawk—a square board with a handle underneath—and tuck it into the joints with a trowel. To achieve a smooth, even finish, press along the partly dried joints with a piece of 15 mm tubing.

Applying Protective Coatings

Preparing for paint. Using a stiff brush, remove any dust or loose material from the surface. If moss, fungus or similiar growths are present, treat the affected areas with a fungicide, making sure that it is compatible with the type of paint you intend to use. Then remove the growths with a stiff brush and scraper. Apply a second coat of fungicide to the surface and allow it to dry. Finally, make good deep cracks or holes and repair defective mortar joints.

If the surface is smooth or only slightly textured, paint may be applied with a conventional brush or roller. However, for a heavily textured surface, such as brick or pebble dash, you should use a roller sleeve with a deep pile or a rough-surface paintbrush *(right)*. The strong fibre filling of this brush will stand up to abrasive surfaces much better than pure bristle.

Charge the brush or roller with plenty of paint and work with slow, smooth strokes, ensuring that any cracks or uneven areas are filled. Do not overstretch the paint—one exterior coat should be twice as thick as an interior coat.

Selecting the right cladding. Timber weatherboarding is widely used as a traditional form of wall cladding. Nailed to a framework of softwood battens, each board overlaps the one below it, thus providing a tight seal against wind and moisture. Fixing is done from the bottom upwards, and two horizontal battens—one laid on top of the other—are screwed to the wall just above ground level to give the first board the correct tilt. Corner battens hold the edges of the boards on adjoining surfaces and architrave battens fitted round door and window openings protect the end grains of the boards.

A more sophisticated alternative is shiplap cladding. The cladding is fixed to a framework of battens, in the same way as weatherboarding, but instead of overlapping, the sections have matching rebates which interlock. This provides extra protection for the joints and extends the life of the nails.

Timber cladding, however, requires regular painting or varnishing to keep up its appearance, and it is likely to warp badly if not thoroughly seasoned. Furthermore, top-grade timber commands a premium price. You might do better, therefore, to choose a tongue-and-groove cladding in ready-coloured aluminium or plastic *(right)*. Both types are cheaper than wood and require virtually no maintenance.

When cladding solid walls, it may be worthwhile applying an insulating material at the same time. Various types are available, including glass fibre mat and polystyrene foam board. But get expert advice on fitting the insulation, and take particular care in detailing round doors and windows and under the eaves.

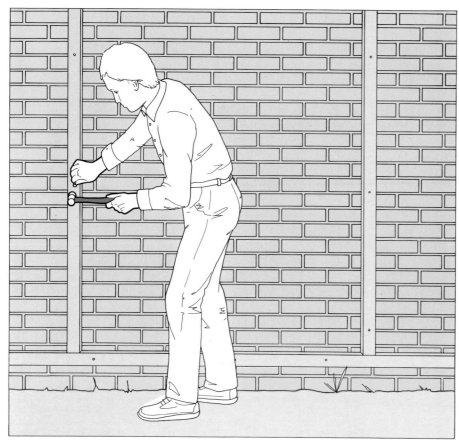

Rendering a Wall

1 **Fixing battens.** Begin by setting out the wall with 10 mm thick softwood battens spaced at intervals of about 1.5 metres. These will guarantee a smooth, level finish for the undercoat and can be removed once it has been applied. Fix the battens with masonry nails driven into the mortar joints, leaving the heads protruding sufficiently to make their removal easy.

To ensure that mortar does not bridge the damp-proof course at the base of the wall, and to achieve a neat edge, fix a batten of the same thickness as the final render—about 15 mm—along the top of the DPC. Also pin battens around the reveals of doors and windows. These should project beyond the reveals by 10 mm to align with the battens on the wall.

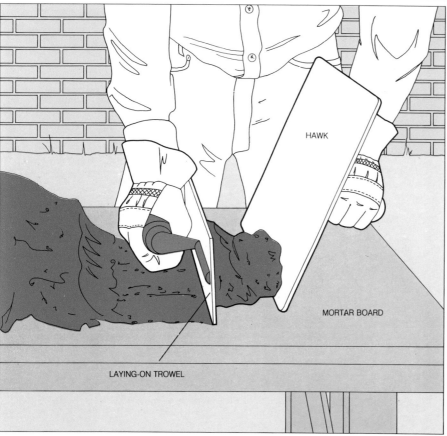

HAWK

LAYING-ON TROWEL

MORTAR BOARD

2 **Preparing the mortar.** To mix the mortar, tip the sand into a wheelbarrow or on to a hard, flat surface such as a sheet of plywood. Add the lime and mix with a hoe or shovel until the ingredients are evenly coloured. Make a well in the centre, tip in the cement and mix once again. Make another well and pour in the water; start with about half the amount by volume of the dry ingredients. Hoe the mortar mixture into the water. Working back and forth, add more water until the mortar has a butter-like consistency and all the lumps are eliminated. Load some of the mortar on to a mortar board supported on a trestle or stool. Scrape about 1 litre of mortar on to a hawk; hold the hawk almost perpendicular to the mortar board *(left)*.

For most building brick, the standard undercoat consists of 1 part Portland cement, 1 part hydrated lime and 5 parts clean, dry plastering sand. You can also use 1 part masonry cement—a blend of cement and lime—to 4 parts plastering sand. On a hard, dense background, such as dense concrete block or very hard brick, the respective ratios should be 1:½:4 and 1:2½. As an alternative to mixing from separate ingredients, you can buy 50 kg bags of dry mortar to which only water need be added. Make sure, however, that the mortar is suitable for the type of wall you are rendering.

If you mix your own mortar, start with a 10 litre bucket of cement and proportionate amounts of sand and lime. You can increase the quantity once you know how much you can comfortably use in a hour—after which time the mortar will start to set.

3 **Applying the mortar.** Holding the hawk level in one hand, separate a slice of mortar with the edge of the trowel. Angle the hawk and use the trowel blade to scoop the slice upwards and push it firmly against the wall. Spread the mortar with smooth, upward sweeps, starting from the edge of the first batten and working gradually across to the next. Repeat until the section of wall between the two battens is filled. Before scooping up each slice of mortar, give the hawk a quarter turn. This will ensure that the load remains centred and evenly balanced.

4 **Smoothing the undercoat.** Once you have filled the wall between the first pair of battens, use the laying-on trowel to smooth and compact the surface. Care taken at this stage will ensure that air bubbles are expelled from the mortar, and that it sticks firmly to the wall.

5 Levelling the undercoat. Using a darby—a long, narrow wooden or metal float—smooth the undercoat level with the battens. If you do not have a darby, you can make one by securing a door handle to a length of clear-grained timber. Fill any depressions in the surface and again slide the darby up and down to remove excess mortar. If the darby drags, allow the mortar to set a while longer and try again.

6 Filling the gaps. After the whole wall has been covered, leave the mortar to dry for about three hours and then carefully remove the vertical battens. Fill in the gaps with mortar and use the laying-on trowel to smooth the new material level with the existing undercoat.

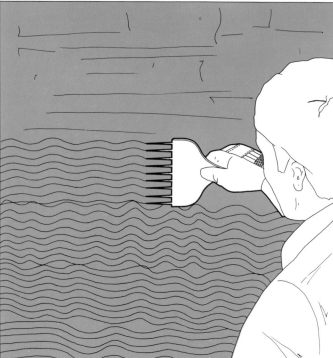

7 Scoring the undercoat. When the undercoat has set hard enough not to be marked with a thumb print, but not too hard to be scratched, score the surface with horizontal wavy lines to create a good key for the topcoat. This can be done with a scratch comb—available from most builders' merchants—or you can make your own tool by hammering nails through a square piece of wood.

Remove the battens round door and window openings and apply a 10 mm thick undercoat to the reveals. After scratch combing, refix the battens so that they overlap the reveals by 5 mm.

The whole wall should then be left to harden for at least a week. In warm, dry weather, dampen the surface regularly with mist spray to help the curing process.

8 **Applying the topcoat.** Mix up enough mortar to give a 5 mm overall covering. Apply the topcoat in the same way as the undercoat, spreading the mortar with firm, upward sweeps, and working from one edge of the wall to the other. Do not use vertical battens for the topcoat as you could damage the undercoat.

Unless the wall is exposed to severe weathering the topcoat should contain proportionately less cement than the undercoat. Use 1 part cement, 2 parts lime and 8 parts sand, or 1 part masonry cement to 5½ parts sand.

When the render has hardened—after at least 24 hours—remove the batten at DPC level and the boards round door and window openings. Then finish the reveals.

9 **Finishing off.** Smooth the rendering with firm, upward sweeps, using the laying-on trowel for a smooth finish and the darby (right) for a gritty finish. Take special care round corners and where reveals meet the outside wall. Avoid overpolishing; this will cause water to separate out from the mortar.

As an alternative, you can produce a textured finish, either by scraping the surface with the edge of a trowel, scratch combing in various patterns or scrubbing with a steel brush.

For increased durability, you can apply a pebble-dash finish immediately after applying the topcoat. Simply load a bucket with pebbles or crushed stones and throw them at the still wet mortar by hand or with a small shovel. Once the mortar dries, the stones are held tightly to provide a durable surface.

Damp-Proof Courses: the Barriers to Rising Damp

Rising damp is one of the most common problems in older houses, indicating either that there is no damp-proof course (DPC) or that an existing DPC has broken down. If the DPC is faulty, make sure, before going to the trouble and expense of installing a new one, that there is not a simpler way of solving the problem.

The first step in dealing with rising damp is to find the DPC. If it is the traditional type, consisting of a layer of slate, lead or copper, there will be an extra-wide mortar course near ground level. If it is a more recent type, made up of flexible black polythene or bitumen sheeting, a thin black line should show through the mortar, also near ground level.

Once you have located the DPC, trace the line around the house to ensure that it is not bridged at any point, either internally or externally *(page 46)*. If there is no DPC, or if the existing one is clearly inadequate, one will have to be installed.

There are only two damp-proof courses that experts regard as being satisfactory. The first type, which involves cutting a slot into a mortar course a section at a time, and then inserting a physical barrier of impermeable material, is best left to a professional. This method is not suited to unusually thick walls or those that are cracked or unstable, and can involve a considerable expenditure of time and money.

The second method—and one that the amateur will find easier to tackle—is to saturate the base of the walls with a proprietary damp-coursing solution. This forms a continuous chemical barrier which interrupts the natural capillary action of the walls and prevents the damp rising; it also dispels the dampness, allowing the wall to dry out by natural evaporation.

Three separate stages are involved in the injection of a damp-coursing solution: drilling entry holes for the fluid; carrying out a preliminary run with water to test for damaged brickwork; and putting in the fluid *(page 47)*. This can either be injected under pressure or introduced by gravity transfusion—in which case the fluid seeps slowly into the walls through tubes connected to special irrigation bottles.

The work is best carried out in late summer, when the water tables are at their lowest and the walls are relatively dry. The drier the walls, the more complete will be the penetration of the solution.

Where internal plasterwork has been affected by damp, this should be stripped away to a height of one metre above the floor and replaced using a chemical neutralizer in the plaster. The neutralizer acts against the moisture and moisture-absorbent mineral salts that will remain in the walls while they dry out—a process that could take up to 12 months.

Mix an undercoat of 1 part Portland cement to 8 parts fine sand with a water-proofer and mortar plasticizer; apply in the same way as rendering *(pages 40–43)*, adding a thin layer of finishing plaster. Wait until the walls have dried out before applying paint or other wall coverings.

Damp-coursing fluid is not only highly inflammable, but it can also injure your eyes and skin. Always wear goggles and heavy-duty gloves when handling it, and do not smoke or use other naked flames. If you are working indoors, ensure that there is plenty of ventilation.

The classic signs of rising damp. Rising damp is indicated by an excessively damp wall base. Often, there is a continuous tide-mark of discoloration, rising to about one metre in most cases. This is due to water carrying soluble salts from the soil into the wall. These salts, which remain firmly embedded in the wall, exacerbate the problem by absorbing further moisture from the surrounding air.

How a DPC Works

The physical damp-proof course. Constructed of impermeable material, a DPC provides a barrier against rising damp in the external walls of a house. To be effective, the course must be continuous and located at least 150 mm above ground level. In cavity-wall construction, the interior leaf is also protected by a DPC, installed at the same height as the one in the exterior leaf. Where the ground floor is a suspended timber one *(top right)*, the joists are supported by sleeper walls and should also be protected from rising damp where the two meet. Where the ground floor is concrete *(bottom right)*, the damp-proof membrane which lies just below the surface must either overlap or extend to become the DPC in the outside wall or, in the case of cavity construction, the inner leaf *(right)*.

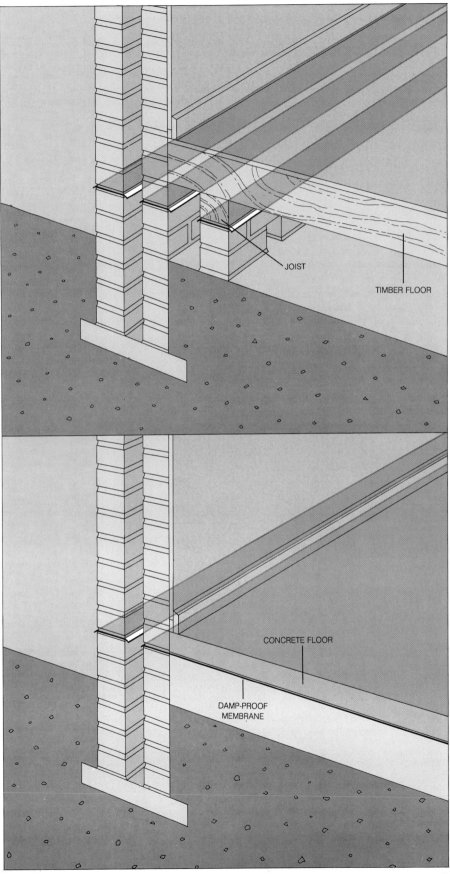

JOIST

TIMBER FLOOR

CONCRETE FLOOR

DAMP-PROOF MEMBRANE

Faulty Damp-Proof Courses

An earth bypass. Moisture will bypass the damp-proof course if earth is heaped against the wall above the line of the course. To remove the bridge, clear away earth until the DPC is at least 150 mm above ground level.

Rendered walls. The DPC will be ineffective if it has been rendered over. If the whole wall is rendered, strip off the rendering from just above the DPC down to the ground level. If only the base is covered, remove the rendering to ground level or 150 mm below the DPC.

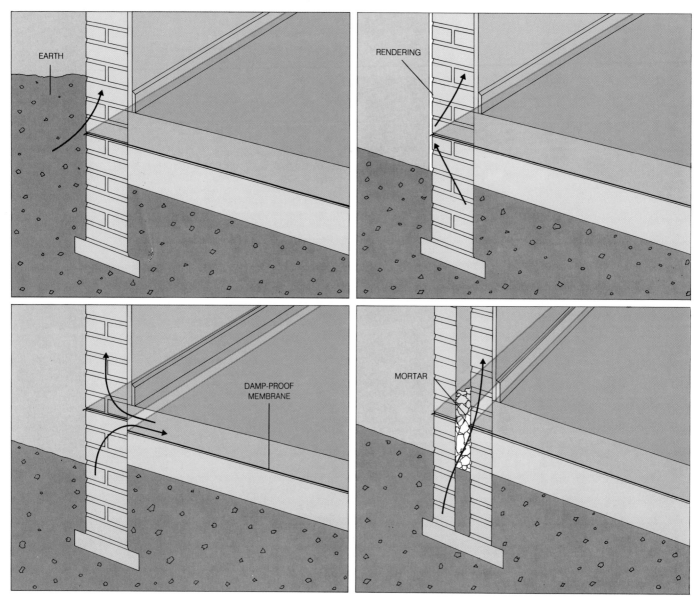

EARTH

RENDERING

DAMP-PROOF MEMBRANE

MORTAR

Interrupted barrier. Where the damp-proof membrane in a solid floor falls below the level of the DPC and the two have not been overlapped, damp is able to creep through the ensuing gap. To remedy this, first cut away the edge of the floor down to the DPC. Then connect the DPC and the floor membrane by placing a vertical membrane overlapping the two on the inner face of the wall. Finally, reinstate the edge of the floor, making certain that the membrane is not pierced when nailing any skirting to the wall.

Bridged cavity. Mortar that has dropped down inside a cavity wall is another frequent cause of dampness. It provides a bridge for rising damp and a conduit for rainwater to cross from the outer to the inner leaf, causing an isolated damp patch. To remove the mortar, chip out a small section of brickwork, no more than a couple of bricks, from the outer leaf above the DPC. This is a delicate task and care must be taken not to weaken the wall by removing too many bricks.

Installing a Chemical DPC

1 Drilling the holes. Use a heavy-duty hammer drill, available from a tool-hire shop, to drill angled holes at the required level. The angle of the holes, as well as their depth, spacing and diameter, should be as recommended by the manufacturers of the damp-coursing solution. Solid walls are normally drilled from one side, but cavity walls may be drilled from one or both sides. If you drill a cavity wall from one side, introduce the damp-course fluid into the near leaf first, then drill through the existing holes into the far leaf and repeat the treatment.

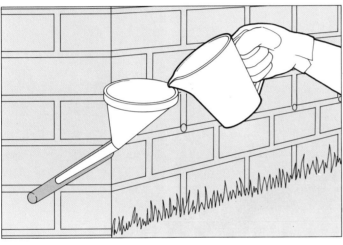

2 Testing for damage. To check that the fluid will not escape through cracks or into voids instead of penetrating the masonry, fill each hole with water, using a 570 ml jug and an offset funnel. If there is a rapid fall in the water level, trace and make good any damage, or else drill another hole next to the one that has failed and fill the original one with mortar. Leave for at least six hours before introducing the damp-coursing fluid.

3 Transfusing the fluid. Make sure that the spouts of the bottles are connected firmly to the tops of the tubes and that the sealing collars of the tubes are fitted tightly round the drill holes. Use a 570 ml jug to fill the bottles with the amount of fluid recommended by the manufacturers and check for any signs of leakage. Do not remove the transfusion units until the wall has been properly saturated, which could take up to three days.

   Allow about three or four weeks for the fluid to dry out and then make good the walls. Holes drilled internally which will be covered by skirting boards should be left unplugged, but external and other visible holes should be filled with a mortar mix of 1 part Portland cement to 3 parts fine sand. Finish off by restoring damaged rendering and plasterwork.

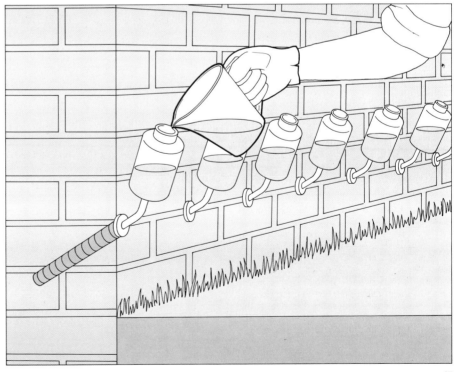

Laying Drains Underground

Even the most careful maintenance of roofs, gutters and walls may leave them vulnerable to dampness if your rainwater disposal system is inadequate. Guttering downpipes are normally connected to the main drains, but in older properties a downpipe may discharge directly on to the ground near the foundation of a house, causing excessive dampness in the surrounding soil. Similar problems may affect a more recent house if a small extension such as a lean-to or an extra room is built, in which case it may not be possible to position the downpipe to discharge directly into the surface-water sewer.

The most effective method of conveying gutter water away from the foundation is through a buried pipe, 75 or 100 mm in diameter, which is attached to the downpipe below ground with an elbow joint. In the past, drainage pipes were traditionally made of earthenware, but modern pipe is made of plastic, which is unbreakable and easier to install. The pipe is laid in a ditch that must be sloped slightly away from the house to allow the water to flow.

Your local water authority or building control officer will advise on the correct gradient, but 25 mm in 1 metre is generally sufficient. To set the gradient, attach a wooden spacer block, 25 mm thick, below one end of a metre-long piece of wood and place a spirit level on top. When the bubble in the spirit level becomes centred, the gradient is correct. The depth of the ditch will depend on its length, but you should allow for a covering of at least 150 mm of topsoil at the house end.

If possible, the pipe should discharge into a surface-water sewer, in which case you must get an expert to make the connection. Alternatively, you can build a soakaway *(overleaf)* or, if your garden slopes towards a stream, you may be able to get permission from your local water authority to use it as an outlet. Bear in mind that all drainage systems are subject to building regulations and other statutory control.

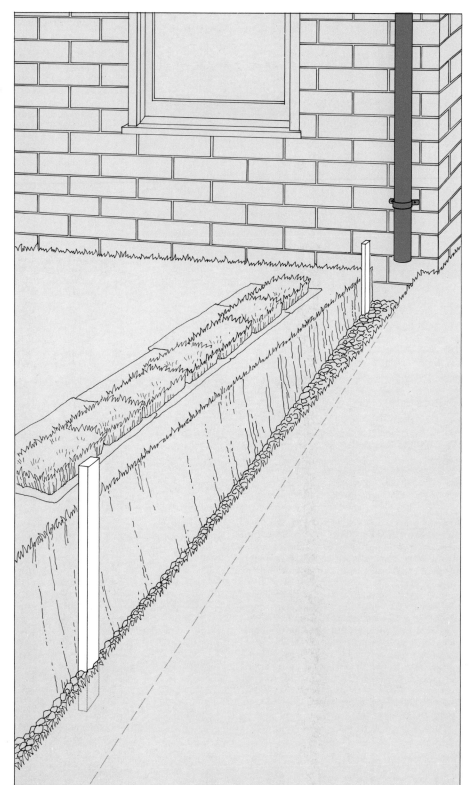

1 **Digging the ditch.** Use a wooden stake to mark each end of the line to be followed by the ditch. Remove 300 mm wide patches of turf between the stakes and lay them, grass side up, next to the ditch. Using a pointed shovel, dig a ditch 250 to 500 mm deep next to the house, inclined to the required depth at the other end. Line the bottom of the ditch with 25 to 50 mm of gravel.

2 **Installing the pipe.** Choose plastic drainpipe to match the existing piping. If you cannot buy the exact length you want, cut the pipe to fit with a hacksaw. The downpipe is connected to the drainpipe with an elbow joint. Many modern joints have "push-fit" seals provided by rubber flanges, but some systems require the application of glue or a solvent and glue before connection. Follow the manufacturer's instructions to ensure that you obtain a water-tight seal. Lay the drainpipe in the ditch. Attach one end of the elbow to the downpipe *(right)* and the other to the drainpipe *(far right)*. Bed the drainpipe, including the connected section, in the gravel.

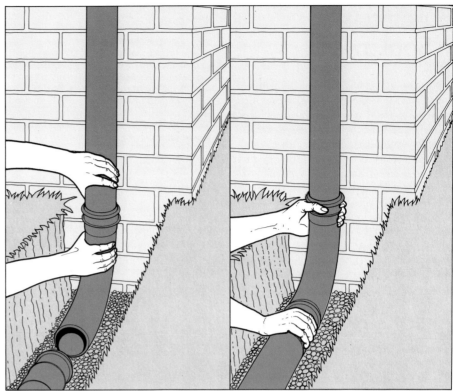

3 **Filling in the ditch.** Starting at the end nearest the house, fill in the ditch. Lay the turf back in place on the surface and gently tamp each piece down with your foot. The slight mound that is created by the pipe will settle in time.

Building a Soakaway

If you are unable to drain rainwater runoff into a surface sewer or stream, the solution may be to build a soakaway—a pit that collects water and lets it slowly percolate into the soil. First, however, check with your local council or water authority that the soil is free-draining and that the level of the subsoil water—known as the water table—is well below the surface.

Some soakaways are huge, cement-lined tanks best left for a contractor to build. But a small soakaway capable of draining a roof area of 20 square metres can easily be made using a standard 200 litre oil drum, or a plastic bin of equivalent size.

Prepare the drum by removing the top and bottom and cutting a hole in its side with a cold chisel as shown on the right. (For a plastic bin, use a utility or trimming knife.) Then select an appropriate site for the soakaway. This should be at least 4.5 metres from the downpipe and should slope away from the house.

Excavating a hole 1.5 metres deep may be difficult in rocky soil. If a pick is not adequate for breaking large stones in the hole, use a sledgehammer.

1 Cutting the drum. Use a cold chisel to remove the top and bottom of the drum and to carve a hole in its side large enough to admit the drainpipe that you have selected. First knock the chisel through the metal with a hammer. Then use the carving edge of the chisel to slice sideways through the drum. Wear gloves and always cut from the outside of the drum. After cutting the pipe hole, use a hammer and chisel to punch small drain holes spaced uniformly round the drum.

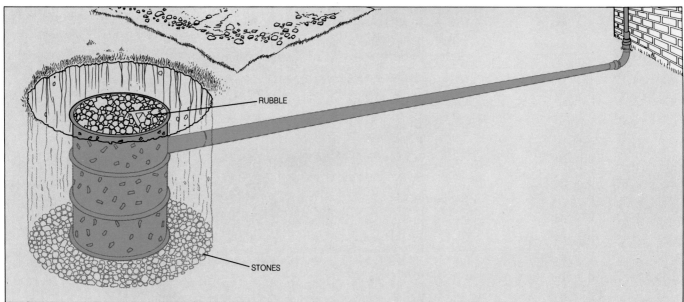

RUBBLE

STONES

2 Placing the drum. Remove and save the turf from an area about 2 metres in diameter. Dig the hole to a depth of 1.5 metres. Line the bottom with 50 to 100 mm of stones and sink the drum into place. Connect the underground drainpipe to the drum through the hole. (The method for installing the drainpipe is shown on pages 48–49.) Fill the drum with large stones, broken brick, or river gravel ranging from 10 to 150 mm in size.

3 **Surrounding with mesh.** Use a 3 metre long, 1.2 metre wide section of 6 or 10 mm galvanized or plastic-coated wire mesh to circle the drum. Using wire cutters, cut a 100 mm wide opening 150 mm into one end of the mesh at the level that the drainpipe enters the drum. At the other end of the mesh, twist on several short pieces of scrap wire for holding the ends of the mesh together. Slide the mesh round the drum, fitting the opening round the pipe, overlapping the ends and tying them together with the pieces of wire.

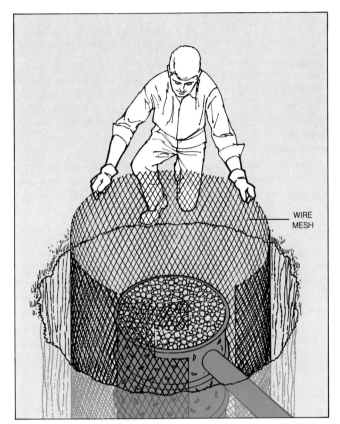

WIRE MESH

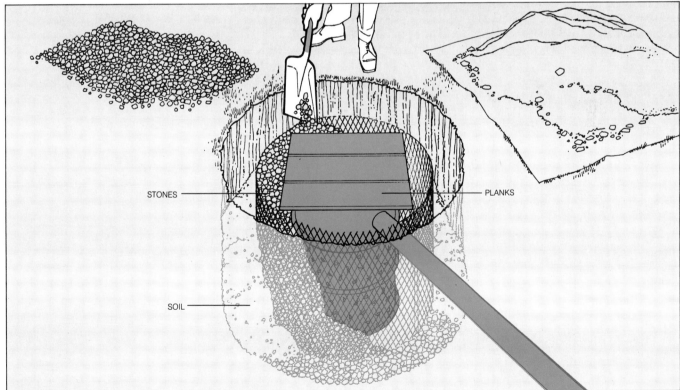

STONES

PLANKS

SOIL

4 **Filling the soakaway.** Cover the top of the drum with 6 or 10 mm wire mesh and sturdy wood planks to prevent earth from entering. Fill the hole, alternately putting stones between the mesh and the drum, and soil between the mesh and the sides of the hole. Filling the gravel first would cause the mesh to open. Cover the soakaway with a layer of gravel and at least 300 mm of soil, then replace the turf.

Choosing the Right Remedy for a Wet Basement

The causes of a wet basement generally lie outside it and, even if the soil round the foundations seems well drained, cracks in basement walls admit water that otherwise would stay outside. Much wetness can be eliminated by fixing interior walls, but work on the exterior may be necessary.

If the basement is damp rather than wet—you see no patches of water but feel excess humidity or see its effects in mildew—the steps are fairly simple. Dampness may arise from water vapour that is generated by appliances in the house such as dishwashers and washing machines—clothes driers are the worst offenders and their exhausts should be vented outdoors (pages 66–67). Paraffin and portable gas heaters also generate water vapour.

Seepage through walls or floor may introduce water as well as humidity, and sometimes humid air generated inside the house may condense into liquid on masonry surfaces, suggesting that moisture is entering from outdoors. To determine whether the problem is inside or outside—and whether ventilation is a sufficient solution—perform the following test. Tape a 400 mm square of heavy plastic sheeting to the wall below ground level. Remove it after several days: dampness underneath means that water is seeping into the basement between grains of sand and cement in a wall that looks solid. If the plastic-covered area is dry and the wall round it is

damp, then water is condensing from moist air that is inside the basement.

If seepage is the problem, there are several ways of dealing with it. Moisture in a moderately damp wall may be blocked with a coat of waterproof cement paint or three coats of bituminous emulsion. Another solution is to render the inside of the wall (below), using a mix of 1 part Portland cement to 3 parts sharp sand and a waterproofing agent, such as silicone or synthetic latex, added according to the manufacturer's instructions. The technique of rendering is shown on pages 40–43.

If you wish to use the basement as a living space, lining the inside of the wall with plasterboard will, at least, prevent damage to decorations, without actually curing the problem, and may be sufficient if the seepage is only moderate. However, make sure that you use pre-treated timber battens and do not place insulation material in direct contact with the damp surface. For really serious seepage, asphalt tanking applied to the outside of the basement walls may be an effective solution, but this necessitates excavation and should be carried out by a professional.

A dirt floor is a common cause of seepage; if you have one, cover it. A polythene sheet will do if you use the basement only rarely. If you use it often, however, lay sturdier concrete covering; follow the procedure described on pages 55–57.

Cracks are more serious than seepage or condensation. They can be caused by settling, infiltrating tree roots and water pressure against walls or floor.

You may first notice a crack on a rainy day as water streams into the basement. The flood can be stopped and the crack fixed by channelling water out through a short hose, then plugging the leak with quick-setting mortar, which hardens on contact with water (page 54).

Once the crisis has passed—or if you discover the crack before it floods the basement—examine the crack carefully. If it is bigger than a hairline, or if a hairline crack becomes visibly wider as time goes on, this may indicate a serious structural fault. Get the advice of a structural engineer before attempting to deal with the problem.

Try repairing stationary cracks from the inside of the basement first (opposite page). If a patch proves ineffective by itself, the crack probably extends through the wall, in which case you must seal the outside of the foundation too. A concrete patch will work for most cracks, but if the exterior wall of the foundation is badly damaged, you will need professional help.

Of all the cracks in a basement, the most troublesome are those that occur where the floor meets the wall. Try filling them with a joint sealer and epoxy resin covered by patching mortar. If this remedy fails, install a sump pump (page 58).

Preventing seepage. Dampen the wall with a moist sponge and trowel on two coats of patching mortar mixed with a waterproofing additive such as silicone or latex. The covering should not exceed 50 mm in total thickness. Work from the floor upwards, forcing the rendering into the junction between the floor and the bottom of the wall. After the mortar dries but before it sets—about one to two hours—use a stiff brush to apply a coat of waterproof cement paint, working the paint into the fresh cement.

PATCHING MORTAR

Filling stationary cracks. Open the crack with a cold chisel *(right)* until it is about 10 mm wide, then remove loose concrete with a wire brush. Fill the crack with a mastic joint sealer or a silicone sealant *(page 18)*, leaving about 15 mm unfilled. Use a pointing trowel to cover the sealant with an epoxy or other resin mortar.

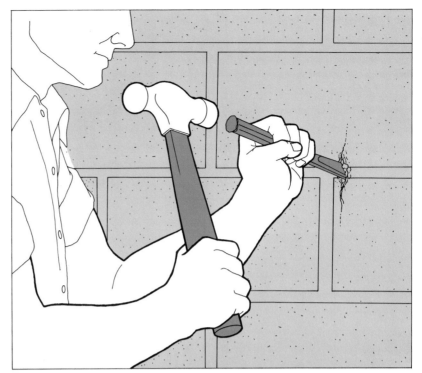

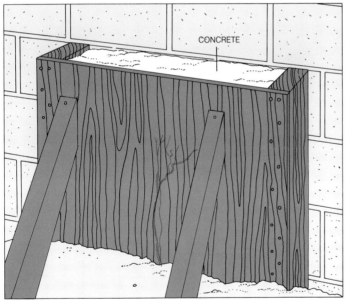

CONCRETE

Small ground-level cracks. Excavate the wall 300 mm below and beyond either side of the crack, then build a three-sided form. Cut 100 by 50 mm pieces of timber long enough to reach between the bottom of the excavation and 300 mm above the crack. Nail to these edges 12 mm plywood the length of the strips and 600 mm wider than the crack. Prop the form over the crack with 100 by 50 mm scraps and fill it with a standard concrete mix. Let the concrete set for about 24 hours before removing the timber form.

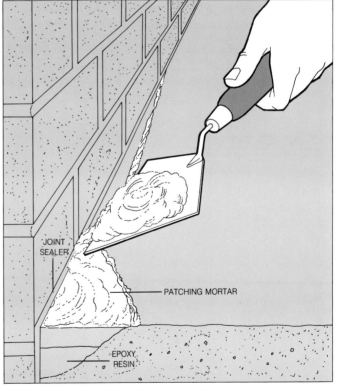

JOINT
SEALER

PATCHING MORTAR

EPOXY
RESIN

Filling wall-floor cracks. Widen the outside of the crack with a cold chisel, making a bevelled slot. Dry the crack with a propane torch and line the slot next to the wall with a strip of mastic or silicone joint sealer 5 mm thick to keep out moisture. Half fill the rest of the slot with epoxy resin mortar to prevent the mastic from loosening, then fill up the slot with patching mortar.

Plugging Flowing Leaks

1 **Inserting a bleeder hose.** Chip loose concrete away from the hole and insert a length of appropriately sized rubber hose so that the water can be diverted into a bucket. Fill round the hole with quick-setting mortar, which hardens within a minute or so of coming into contact with water. It is available from most hardware shops.

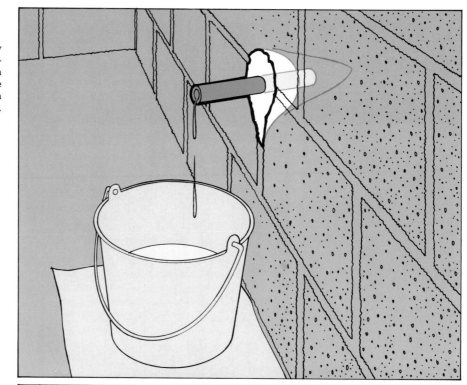

2 **Inserting a plug.** When the space round the bleeder hose has been filled, pull out the hose and use a dowel or metal rod to ram quick-setting mortar into the remaining gap, holding the plug firmly in place until it has set.

A Damp-Proof Solid Floor

Although most modern houses have solid concrete floors at ground level, suspended timber floors are very common in older properties, and are one of the first areas to be affected by damp. Often, the resulting damage can be repaired *(pages 118–121)*. Where this is not possible, however, the most effective long-term solution is to replace the timber floor with one of concrete. Consult the appropriate authorities regarding the protection of exposed electric cables and gas and water pipes. Heating and water pipes should be lagged; cables should be re-routed or enclosed in conduits.

The diagram on the right shows the best form of construction for a solid floor. The bottom layer consists of builders' rubble from which absorbent materials, such as plaster scraps and paper, have been removed. Next comes a "blinding" layer of firmly tamped sand or hoggin (sandy clay). This is covered, in turn, by a damp-proof membrane of polythene or polythene-bitumen "sandwich" sheet. Installed so that its edges lie flush with the walls, overlapping the DPC, the membrane provides an all-round barrier against rising damp.

The membrane itself is covered by a concrete slab, and above the slab a cement-based screed forms a smooth, level surface. The floor can usually be walked on after a week or so, but make sure it has thoroughly dried before putting down a covering. Allow 30 days for every 25 mm of slab and screed thickness.

The membrane should not be laid directly under the screed. This would place too great a stress on the membrane and could result in its failure. Where the membrane becomes inoperative, or where a solid floor has been laid without membrane, moisture from the ground can pass through the concrete, causing damp and mould to collect under carpets and other coverings.

In this case, the simplest remedy is to treat the surface with a waterproofing compound, such as rubberized bitumen, which should be applied in three coats. A more durable solution is to apply a waterproofer directly to the concrete, which should then be covered with a new screed at least 65 mm thick. A screed laid on top of the existing one will cause problems with doors and other fittings.

Construction of a solid floor. A solid floor consists of a number of layers of different materials. The foundation is made up of builders' rubble or hardcore and is usually 100 to 150 mm thick, depending on the final floor level. Blinding, a thin layer of sand or hoggin spread on top of the hardcore to bind it, forms a firm base for the damp-proof membrane, which is followed by a concrete floor slab the same thickness as the hardcore. The slab is then coated with grout to provide a bond with the topmost layer—a mortar screed about 40 mm thick.

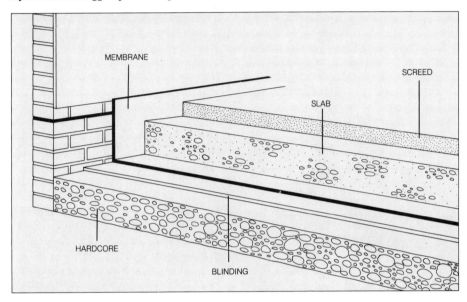

Laying a Concrete Floor

1 Breaking up the hardcore. Remove skirting boards, floorboards and joists, and make sure that any underfloor wires or pipes are properly protected. Lay the hardcore in place, breaking up any large or jagged pieces with a sledgehammer, and compact it as tightly as possible into a layer 100 to 150 mm thick.

2 Laying the blinding. Shovel a layer of sand, hoggin or fine ash to completely cover the hardcore, then smooth and compress it with a length of wood. The blinding will provide a firm surface for the damp-proof membrane and protect it from the sharp edges of the hardcore.

3 Installing the membrane. Cut away plaster up to a point about 25 mm higher than the DPC. Cover the blinding layer with 250 micron (1000-gauge) polythene or polythene-bitumen sheeting, folding up the edges so that they overlap the DPC in the exposed brickwork. Tuck the sheet neatly into the corners and smooth out any wrinkles. Lap any joints and seal them with heavy-duty PVC tape.

4 Laying the floor slab. Mark on the wall the required surface level of the slab. Lay the concrete in strips about 1 metre wide, filling in first along the side of the room opposite the door, then the two adjacent sides and finally down the centre towards the doorway. Use a rake to spread the concrete to about 10 mm above the required level and tamp with a 100 by 50 mm board *(left)*. Check levels with a straightedge and spirit level; minor variations will be filled in by the screed.

To estimate how many cubic metres of concrete you need, simply multiply the area to be covered by the thickness of the slab. Use a mix of 1 part Portland cement to 2 parts concreting sand and 3 parts of 20 mm maximum size coarse aggregate, or 1 part cement to 4 parts of 20 mm maximum size "all-in" aggregate. Mix as for mortar *(page 40)*, first blending the dry ingredients and then adding water. For large quantities, hire a mixer.

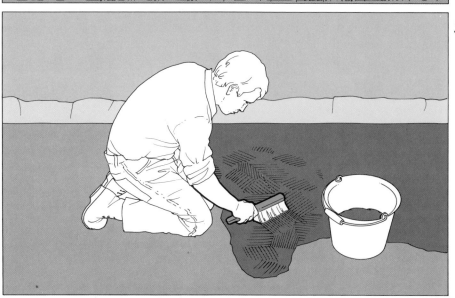

5 Grouting the floor slab. Allow the concrete to harden until it is firm enough to walk on, then scrub it down thoroughly with warm water and a stiff broom to remove fine particles from the surface. Cover the concrete with damp sacking or plastic sheeting and leave it to cure for three days. Grout immediately after this time to ensure a good bond.

Dampen the floor slab with water and apply the grout with a soft brush, working down the room in strips about 1 metre wide. Follow the same pattern you used for the slab, starting at the sides of the room and finishing off with the centre, working towards the door. As you complete each strip, go on directly with Steps 6 to 8.

To make the grout, mix cement and water to the consistency of double cream then add a proprietary bonding compound in the proportion recommended by the manufacturer.

6 **Fixing the screeding rails.** Once you have finished grouting the first strip, fix screeding rails to mark out the final floor level. Use 1 metre lengths of timber and, with the aid of a hammer, bed them in well compacted mortar laid along the outside of the strip. Check with a spirit level and straightedge that the rails are level. Repeat the same procedure for subsequent strips.

To make the screeding mortar, use 1 part ordinary Portland cement to 3 parts sharp sand (not bricklayer's sand), or 1 part cement to 4 parts sharp sand if the screed is to be covered with rigid tiles. Mix and apply, following the method described on page 40. Check the consistency of the mortar by squeezing a little in your hand—it should be wet enough for a little water to escape, but dry enough not to crumble.

7 **Levelling the screed.** Lay the screed in strips about 1 metre wide, levelling and smoothing one section before moving on to the next. Spread the mortar to about 7 mm above the final level, then tamp with a 100 by 50 mm board. Take care not to disturb the screeding rails.

When the mortar has been thoroughly compacted, strike off the excess by sliding the tamping beam along the screeding rails *(right)*. If there is no excess, you have used too little mortar; lay some more, compact and strike off again.

If you are working along a side of the room, where only a single line of screeding rails has been set up, lay one end of the tamping beam on the rails, and rest the other end against the exposed wall surface.

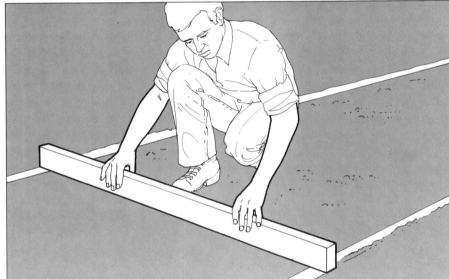

8 **Smoothing the surface.** As you level each of the outer strips, remove the previous line of screeding rails and fill in the depressions with fresh mortar. Follow the same procedure for the centre strip, but this time remove the rails from both sides. Compact the freshly laid mortar with the tamping beam, then smooth the surface with a wooden float *(right)*.

When the screed has become hard enough to walk on, cover it with plastic sheeting and leave it to cure for three days. Tiles can be laid about two weeks thereafter, but allow extra time for the screed and floor slab to dry out thoroughly if you are applying a flexible floor covering.

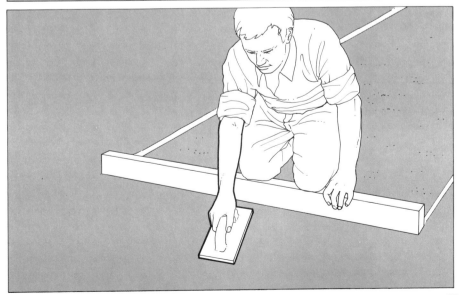

If All Else Fails, a Sump Pump

In some cases the best solution to a wet-basement problem is not sealing the foundation walls but installing a sump pump that will expel water as fast as it enters. A sump pump may be preferable to expensive foundation repairs if, for example, basement flooding only occurs infrequently during severe storms. And it is the only practical remedy if water is being forced up through the basement floor by a rising water table. In addition to solving immediate problems, a sump pump is good insurance against water damage from burst pipes or backed-up basement drains.

Sump pumps are available in many different versions. Most are permanently installed units that run on electricity, but they may also be powered by small diesel engines or by pressure from the water mains, and they are sometimes intended for occasional emergency duty rather than regular use. Sump pumps empty water that runs into a hole, or sump, that must be dug in the lowest part of the basement. The pump starts automatically as the water level in the sump rises, then switches itself off when the water has been evacuated.

Installing a sump pump is an interdisciplinary task, typically calling for the skills of a plumber, an electrician and a carpenter. The first part of the job is to dig the sump. To chop through the concrete floor of most basements, you can hire a pneumatic drill from a tool hire shop. The sump will have to accommodate a liner—a bottomless cylinder, available from plumbing suppliers in a variety of materials, that prevents the sides of the hole from caving in. A liner should have a diameter of at least 400 mm; a smaller liner with less water capacity will shorten the life of a pump by causing it to operate more frequently. Before purchasing the liner, check the pump manufacturer's instructions for any recommendations on diameter and depth.

In making plans for a discharge pipe, first consult your local authority. Most local councils will not allow you to pump basement water into sewer drains, but many will not object if you pipe the water to the storm drain system. Or you can simply pump the water away from the house and let it disperse through the soil. Sump pumps usually require discharge piping with a 30 or 40 mm diameter. Use plastic pipe if possible; it is easier to work with.

Manufacturers of electric sump pumps usually recommend that power be drawn from a separate, unswitched outlet. Such a source can safely supply the large amounts of current that are required to start most sump pumps, and it will also ensure that the pump cannot be unintentionally disconnected by turning off the basement light switch. Before installing a new socket for the pump, check your local electricity regulations to be sure that you use the correct materials. Call in a professional electrician to make the necessary connection at the fuse board.

Every pump should have a cover in order to keep out pump-clogging debris and eliminate the possibility of injuries caused by unexpectedly stepping into an open hole. Some sump liners can be purchased with a ready-made cover, but in most cases you will have to make your own.

Two common pumps. Electric sump pumps are available in two basic forms—pedestal *(below, left)* and submersible *(below, right)*. Both have a rotary pump unit that rests on the floor of the sump. Water enters through a grille, which traps objects that could damage the pump, and leaves from an outlet to which a discharge pipe is attached. The submersible pump, sealed against water and installed below the floor of the basement, is quieter than a pedestal model, which has a less expensive, unsealed motor on top of a long stalk that keeps it above water level. A float near the base of the stalk is connected to a switch that turns on the motor when the water rises above a predetermined level; a submersible pump is controlled by a switch inside the motor.

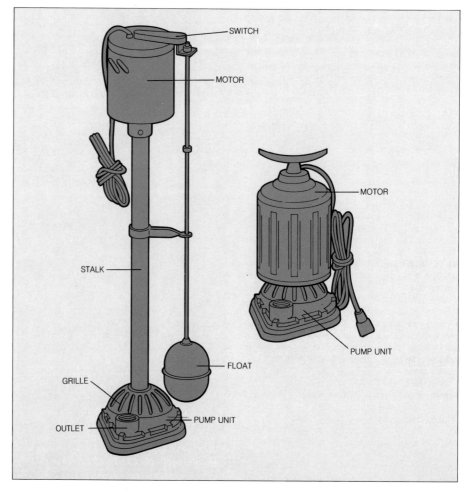

SWITCH

MOTOR

MOTOR

STALK

PUMP UNIT

FLOAT

GRILLE

OUTLET

PUMP UNIT

Coping with the Chaos of a Flood

Clearing Out Mud and Debris

There is not much you can do to protect your house against flood water. If you live in an area where flooding is a possibility—near a river or on a low-lying stretch of coast, for example—you can only hope that weather conditions remain relatively calm. If flooding does occur, however, and you have some advance warning—as you probably will—you can limit the damage to some extent. Once the flood has subsided, there are a number of things you can do to reduce the chaos left in its wake.

When the radio gives the necessary alert, move upstairs as many household effects as you can. Then switch off all gas and electrical appliances and turn off the electricity supply at the mains. Just before you leave the house, open the doors and windows to the basement so that water can enter there to balance the outside pressure and thus prevent a cave-in.

After the flood, when the authorities advise that it is safe to return home, your first priority must be to get rid of any water still trapped in the building. If you call the fire brigade, they will either come and pump it out for you or put you in contact with your local council emergency service. Once this is completed, you should arrange for your gas, water and electrical services to be tested and, if necessary, repaired.

You can then start to clean up the house.

Shifting furniture from room to room or outdoors as you go, remove the silt deposit and debris as shown here. If mud or debris is clogging the DPC, this should be cleared away as soon as possible, otherwise it will prevent the walls from drying out. Remove any mud that has collected under floorboards or inside cavity walls.

As soon as clean water is available, flush out the silt residue with a hose, then wash and disinfect the house and its contents. After that you probably can move back in, but you must delay repainting and refurnishing until everything is dry—a process that may take months.

Meanwhile, you should provide as much heating and ventilation as possible. Leave the doors and windows open, even where fires are lit or heaters are used, and lift the floorboards next to the walls to increase underfloor air flow. Special heaters can be hired to speed up the drying process.

If you have impermeable wall coverings, such as vinyl, these should be stripped off since they could slow down the drying rate. Furniture and pictures should be kept clear of affected walls for the same reason.

As the walls dry out, efflorescence, or white salt growth, will probably appear. This is not harmful and it should stop once all the moisture has evaporated. Simply brush it off as it appears.

1 **Scraping up mud.** Scrape mud off the floors and walls, making sure that all air bricks and ventilators are cleared. Then push the accumulated debris towards a window or outside door with a shovel or a squeegee made by fitting a length of garden hose over the teeth of a rake.

2 **Disposing of mud.** The easiest way to dispose of mud and debris from the ground floor is to slide it down a V-shaped trough propped against the window sill. To make a trough, you need two pieces of timber, each about 25 mm thick, 300 mm wide and 2 metres long. Nail the two pieces together to form a V-shape, then nail a third piece, 50 mm thick and 100 mm wide, under the outside of one end to hold the trough slightly away from the ground.

Once the house is cleared of mud, remove any carpets or loose tiles from the floors and hose away the silt residue. Then scrub the floors and walls with household detergent and disinfectant. As a safeguard against health hazards, you should also arrange for underfloor spaces to be sprayed with disinfectant. Your local authority may be able to assist you with this or they will direct you to a commercial company.

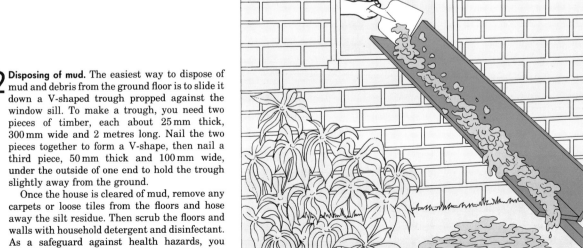

The Indispensable Openings: Vents for Air Flow

To the untrained eye, it may appear that the only openings in a house are the doors and windows. In fact, a well-constructed house will also include a number of ventilation openings to ensure a constant exchange between the warm, moist air inside and the cooler, drier air outside and prevent the accumulation of water vapour.

In the case of a cellar or the space beneath a suspended timber floor, for example, it is essential to provide ventilation through strategically placed grilles or air bricks let into the wall *(page 65)*.

Attic venting is also of prime importance. An unventilated attic is a year-round problem, even if it is insulated from the rest of the house. On hot summer days, attic temperatures can rise dramatically, keeping the rest of the house hot long after the sun has set and in hot climates putting a heavy—and expensive—load on air conditioners. In winter, there is a risk of water vapour rising from other parts of the house

and condensing on the cold underside of the roof covering. If excessive, this moisture can permeate the ceiling and roof structure, rotting timber and damaging insulation and plasterwork.

A steady flow of air through the attic, provided by a combination of the vents shown below, solves both problems by removing hot air in the summer and water vapour in the winter. Ventilation openings should, wherever possible, be at eaves level on opposite sides of the house, to allow cross-ventilation of the attic. Most of these vents are easily installed. Gable vents are fitted in the same way as air bricks or grilles. Ridge tiles and ventilation tiles should be installed by a professional. For ventilation tiles, which should be of the same size and quality as the existing tiles, a hole is cut through the roofing felt with a sharp knife to allow the passage of air.

If practical to install, vents in the soffit—the underside of the roof edge—are

effective. If there are no soffits, ventilation holes may be cut into the fascia board. Where cross-ventilation is not practicable—in mono-pitch roofs, for example—high level venting should be used in conjunction with venting of the eaves. This permits fresh air to enter the attic at a low level and rise, carrying heat or moisture up to be expelled through vents in the gables, the roof ridge or in the roof itself.

The overall area of venting needed for a roof with a pitch of more than 15 degrees is equivalent to a continuous opening on each side at least 10 mm wide. If the pitch is less than 15 degrees, more venting is needed, equivalent to an opening not less than 25 mm. The high vents of a mono-pitch roof should be equivalent to a continuous opening of 5 mm. Vents can be sited irregularly as long as this does not create stagnant areas. All vents should be designed so that they do not allow the entry of rain or snow, birds or small rodents.

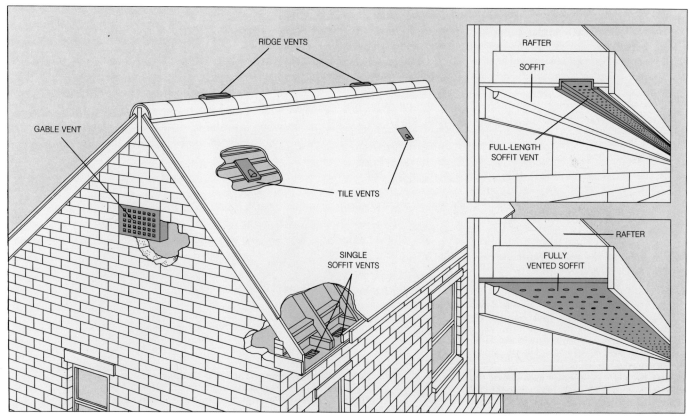

A full range of roof vents. No single house would be fitted with all the openings in this drawing, which is meant as a general guide to the vents described here. Soffit vents fit into the wooden panel, or soffit, that covers the underside of

eaves. The single type is easiest to install, but the full-length strip type is more effective; most effective of all is the fully vented soffit, which has openings over the entire soffit area. Rectangular gable vents, often used in combination

with soffit vents, are set into a wall near the peak of the roof. Tile vents are set into the roof in place of ordinary tiles, while ridge vents are set into the roof at its highest point, where the rafters are joined to the ridge beam.

Installing a single soffit vent. Make a cardboard template matching the part of the vent that will fit into the soffit. Locate a section of the soffit between two soffit bearers—you can identify their positions by the exposed heads of the nails that fasten the soffit to the bearers—and use the template to mark cutting lines for the vent holes. Drill a hole at the corners of the outline as starting points for a keyhole saw, then cut along the lines. Screw the vent to the soffit.

Installing a fully vented soffit. For a fully vented soffit you must remove the existing soffit, which is held in place mainly by nails that are driven through and into the soffit bearers, although it may also rest on a strip of moulding at the top of the wall and against a fascia board at the edge of the roof. You may not have to remove the moulding or the board to take the soffit out. Cut access holes between the soffit bearers, then prise the soffit from the bearers with a hammer and chisel. Free the outer edge of the soffit first, so that you can swing it below the fascia board, then pull an entire section off the top of the moulding. Replace the section with a fully vented soffit, nailing each section to the soffit bearers.

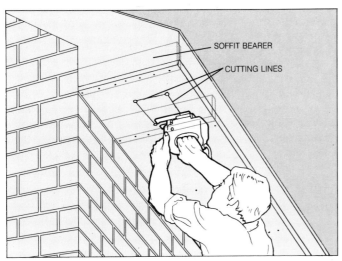

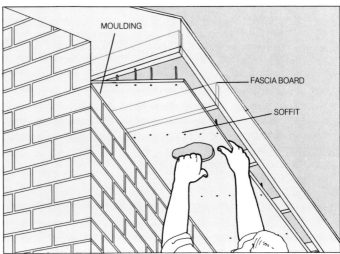

Installing a Strip Vent

1 Marking the vent's position. At each end of the soffit, make a mark about 75 mm in from the roof edge. Snap a chalk line between the two marks as the outer cutting line for the vent. Measuring in from the chalk line, make two additional marks at a distance equal to the width of the part of the vent that will fit into the soffit. Between the marks, snap a second chalk line.

2 Cutting the channel. Cut along the chalk lines between soffit bearers. Make cuts between the lines to remove a soffit strip, leaving only the parts nailed to the bearers. Cut into each piece along the chalk lines and prise it loose with a chisel. Slip each vent section into the channel and nail it to the bearers. If the bearers prevent a good fit, chisel out enough to seat the vent.

Expelling Moisture from the Kitchen, Bathroom and Laundry

Most of the moisture that collects inside a house is in the form of water vapour that arises from activities such as cooking, bathing and clothes drying. Indeed, it has been estimated that a family of four can release as much as 15 litres of water a day into the atmosphere.

In a poorly insulated house a great deal of moisture escapes harmlessly through walls and cracks. But when you tighten your home against the weather, you seal off these escape routes. The moisture accumulates in the air, condenses on walls and windows, and can cause peeling paint, sticky drawers and mildew. To solve the problem, force water vapour out of the house by installing extractor fans in the rooms where it is generated—kitchen, bathroom and laundry. If the clothes drier is in a separate room, then you can simply connect a duct between the drier and a vent let into the wall or window *(pages 66–67)*.

A fan is rated according to the diameter of its impeller and its revolutions per minute (rpm). The bigger the impeller and the faster it rotates, the greater the volume of air the fan can extract in an hour. To calculate the size of the fan you need, work out the volume of the room (length × width × height), then multiply that figure by the number of air changes required each hour. In a kitchen, the number should be about 15, in a bathroom 10.

You can obtain a fan for fitting in either a wall or window. The advantage of a window fan is that it can be as much as 20 per cent cheaper than a similar wall fan; it is also easier to install. On the other hand, you have more choice about where to position a wall fan and so have a better chance of extracting water vapour at its source.

Whichever type you choose, make sure that it is fitted as high up as possible. Make sure, too, that there is an adequate supply of air to replace the air the fan extracts. This is especially important where a kitchen has a flued boiler. The ideal arrangement is to fit the fan opposite a door or window so that the incoming air is drawn across the room.

Installing a wall fan should take only a few hours. Having decided where you want to place the fan, first drill through the entire wall thickness with a long masonry bit and check that there are no internal obstructions such as water pipes or electricity

cables. Using the drill hole as a guide, pencil the position of the fan lining on the wall. The basic steps for fitting the fan are described opposite; bear in mind, however, that the exact procedure will vary from model to model, so you should follow the manufacturer's instructions.

The most daunting part of the installation is likely to be the wiring up, and you would be well advised to leave this to an electrician—even where the law allows you to do it yourself. The wall fan is powered by a cable which runs from a fused connection unit and along a channel cut in

the wall. Where the fan has a special control unit for varying the speed and air-flow direction, the cable goes to the control unit, and separate wiring goes from the unit to the fan. In the case of a simple one-speed extractor, such as the window fan shown overleaf, the connection can be made via a flex and plug to a nearby socket outlet. If no socket exists, have one installed. All electrical work in the house must comply with the wiring regulations issued by the Institution of Electrical Engineers (I.E.E.); if you have any doubts, get a qualified electrician to do the job for you.

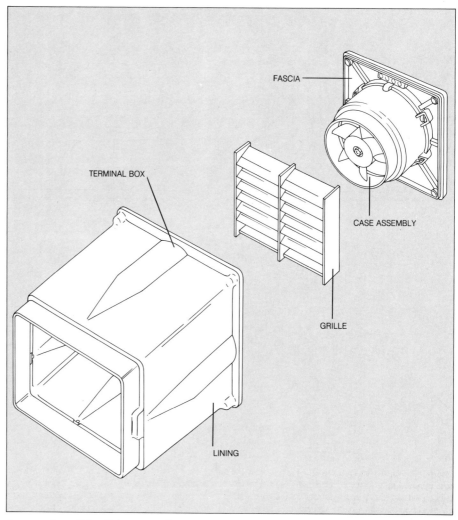

Anatomy of a wall fan. Taken apart for installation, the components in this drawing fit into a hole cut through the wall. Once the lining is in place, the grille slides into it to fit flush with the outside wall. A terminal block, fixed into the terminal box at the top of the lining, is wired to either a wall-mounted control unit or a switched/fused connection unit. The case assembly containing the motor and impeller, fitted to the rear of the fascia, is slipped inside the lining and the fascia, held by a screw at each corner, is mounted over the front of the fan.

Fitting an Extractor Fan in a Wall

1 **Making the opening.** With a hammer and cold chisel, chip away the plaster inside the pencilled outline of the lining (*below*). If necessary, adjust the outline to fall along a mortar line. To remove the first brick from the centre of the outline, chisel round the mortar and gently work out the brick. Continue to remove the bricks in the same way. When removing part of a brick, work from the top; strike downwards into the bricks, not face on. Wear safety goggles to protect your eyes from flying particles.

2 **Fixing the fan lining.** Place the lining in the wall opening (*below*), making sure that the cable entry hole and terminal box are in the position stipulated by the manufacturer. Secure the lining by pointing around the sides with mortar, then clip the grille into position.

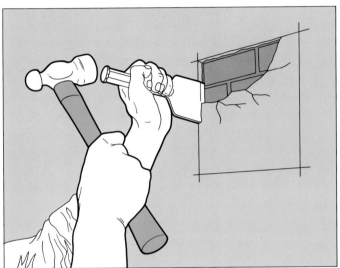

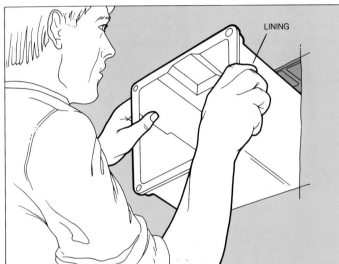

LINING

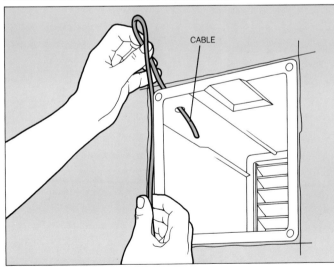

CABLE

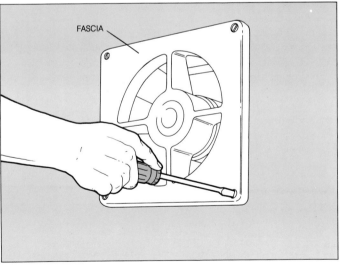

FASCIA

3 **Inserting the cable.** Mark the wall where the cable is to run and make a channel with a hammer and cold chisel. At this point you may wish to consult an electrician. One end of the cable is inserted through the hole in the fan lining (*above*) and wired to the terminal box, while the other end is taken to either a control unit or a switched/fused connection unit. Where the fan has a control unit, this must be separately wired to the connection unit.

4 **Fitting the fascia.** Once the wiring has been completed, make good the plaster chiselled away for the cable channel, then fit the case assembly and fascia into position. Finally, screw the fascia into either the fan lining or the wall, depending on the type of fan (*above*).

Fitting an Extractor Fan in a Window

1 **Scoring a circle.** Prepare to cut a circular hole in the glass by using a circular glass cutter, which consists of a suction pad, a radius scale and a cutting edge that rotates on a pivot. Set the cutting edge to the required radius of the hole, press the suction pad against the centre of the pane and rotate the pivot to score the circle outline. Tap the cut gently from outside to open the score, but do not try to remove the circle from the pane in one piece. Using the same technique, score and tap a second circle about 20 mm inside the first *(below)*.

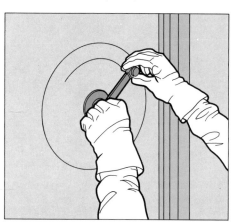

2 **Removing the glass.** Score the inner circle with criss-cross lines. From inside, support the scored glass with a hammer while outside a helper taps out the segments with the ends of the cutter. When all the segments have been removed, score lines between the outer circle and the hole and tap out the remaining pieces of glass. Use pincers to trim round the hole. Always wear thick leather gloves when handling glass and put on safety goggles before cutting.

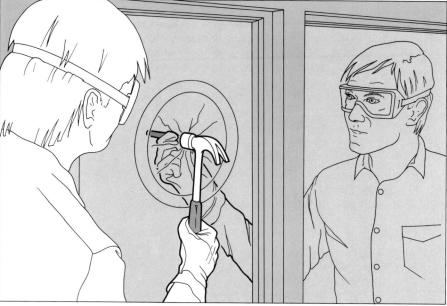

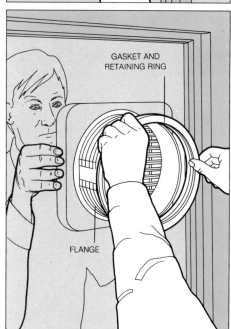

3 **Securing the outer grille.** Get your helper to fit the flange of the outer grille into the window opening from outside; he can then hold the grille steady against the pane while you screw the gasket and retaining ring on to the flange from inside *(above)*. Make sure the grille is the correct way up; the slats should point downwards and outwards to keep out dust and rainwater.

GASKET AND RETAINING RING

FLANGE

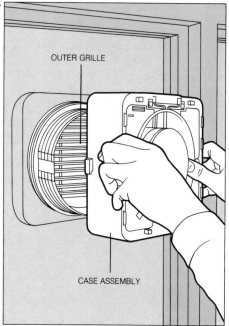

4 **Fitting the casing.** Fit the casing, containing the fan motor and impeller, over the flange *(above)*. Fix the casing into place according to the manufacturer's instructions.

OUTER GRILLE

CASE ASSEMBLY

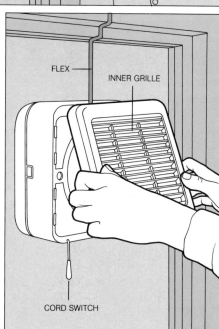

5 **Wiring the fan.** Connect the flex to the terminal block, then clip the block into position at the top of the casing. Take the flex up the window to the frame. Where the fan has a cord switch, as shown here, make sure that the cord is hanging freely from the bottom of the casing before clipping the front grille into place.

FLEX

INNER GRILLE

CORD SWITCH

Airing a Dank Basement

Even after you have eliminated all leaks and seepage *(pages 52–54)*, you may still find that there is moisture in the basement or underfloor area. If this space is unventilated and unheated—and especially if the basement has a dirt floor—moisture condenses on joists and the undersides of floorboards, and spreads upwards inside the house walls. Covering a dirt floor with a polythene membrane *(page 56)* is the essential first step to cure this problem. But if your basement or underfloor area lacks ventilation, it is also necessary to install ventilators. With a membrane laid down, most experts recommend installing one ventilator for every 30 or so square metres of floor area.

Install the ventilators near the top of the foundation walls and close to the corners, but not right next to them. There should be a minimum of two ventilators positioned in opposite walls of the basement. On the rare occasions when more than two ventilators are needed, distribute them at equal intervals in all the walls.

In a cold climate you will need to insulate the underside of the ground floor *(page 86)* if it has not already been done. Outside air in winter is drier than in summer, so you can reduce air circulation and still get rid of unwanted moisture by partially closing ventilators—but leave some opening.

Mortaring the ventilator. Using a chisel and hammer, make an opening in the foundation wall slightly larger than the ventilator. If you expose the hollows inside concrete blocks, pack them with paper to within 25 mm of the surface and fill them the rest of the way with mortar. Let it cure for 24 hours. Half way back and on the bottom of the opening, lay a bead of mortar the width of the ventilator and 20 mm high. Place the ventilator on the mortar and then pack mortar round the other edges of the ventilator with a joint filler or a blunt kitchen knife.

Making a coping. So that rainwater does not accumulate on the sill outside or inside the ventilator, build up a coping, or sloping surface, on both sides of the ventilator. Trowel mortar up to the bottom of the ventilator and then slant it towards the edge of the wall. Place damp rags on the mortar and leave it to cure for 24 hours.

A Clothes-Drier Exhaust Duct

A clothes drier dumps 3 to 4 litres of vaporized water into a laundry room with every average load—enough moisture to cause damage in most houses. To discharge this exhaust outdoors, you need to hook up a special clothes-drier vent before setting the drier into its permanent position. Such vents come in kits that consist of a flexible plastic duct, clamps and a hood vent pipe. Make sure you get one that will fit your drier's exhaust outlets, and get a vent pipe to suit the installation you plan.

Driers can be vented through a window *(right)* with an 80 mm long pipe, or through a wall *(opposite)* with a pipe of suitable dimensions for the wall. The method you choose will depend on the design and construction of your house as well as where you put the clothes drier. The window vent is easiest to install. Simply replace one pane of glass with a vent plate bored to hold the pipe. Pre-bored vent plates are available in transparent plastic or in aluminium. However, you can make your own out of a scrap of 6 mm exterior plywood and then paint it the same colour as the window frame, or you can cut a hole in the existing pane of glass *(page 64)*.

If you do not have a convenient window, or if your windows are close to plants that the exhaust would parch, you will need a wall vent. This requires making a large hole through the foundation of concrete block or brick. Either job is fairly simple with an electric drill.

For efficient venting, the duct should always be as short and straight as possible. Although a plastic duct can bend to snake round pipes or joists, and extra units may be added for stretches of more than the kit's usual 6 metres, loops and long distances slow down the air flow and may cause the duct to clog with lint.

VENT PLATE

VENT PIPE

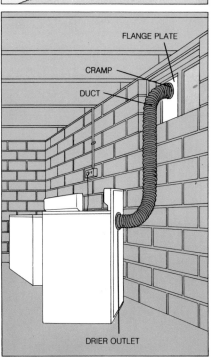

FLANGE PLATE

CRAMP

DUCT

DRIER OUTLET

Installing a Vent in a Window

1 **Attaching the vent plate.** Chisel out the putty round one pane of glass, prise out the glazing points and remove the pane. Wearing goggles, use a hacksaw to cut the vent plate to fit the window opening. Then, working from outside the house, set the plate into the opening. Anchor the plate with glazing points and seal the edges with putty *(left)*. Nail the window shut so that it cannot be opened accidentally.

To make a plywood vent plate, use the pipe as a template for drawing a circle of the required size on the wood. Cut out the circle with a keyhole saw, then trim the plywood to fit the window opening. Follow the procedures above for removing the glass and installing the plate.

2 **Inserting the vent pipe.** Slide off the flange plate from the back of an 80 mm long vent pipe. Working from outside the house, push the pipe through the hole in the vent plate until the back of the hood is flush with the plate.

3 **Attaching the duct.** From inside the house, slip the flange plate over the back of the pipe and press it firmly against the vent plate. Place a cramp on one end of the duct, then fit the duct over the pipe and anchor it by tightening the cramp. Move the drier to its permanent place and extend the duct to the exhaust outlet on the drier. Use scissors or wire cutters to cut off excess duct. Slide a cramp round the loose end of the duct, slip the duct over the drier exhaust outlet and tighten the cramp.

To prevent the duct from sagging, anchor it with string tied to nails in the wall or ceiling joists, or with perforated metal straps held in shape by nuts and bolts and nailed in place.

Installing a Vent in Masonry

1 **Making the opening.** Locate the exhaust opening close to the drier, but away from pipes and shrubs, and outline it with masking tape, indoors and out, in a circle the same diameter as the vent pipe. Wearing goggles, use a 10 or 12 mm masonry bit in an electric drill to bore several holes in the circle from outside, penetrating to the hollow core. Knock out the material between the holes with a hammer and cold chisel *(right)*. Chip away the edges of the opening until it is large enough for the pipe. Then bore and chisel out the opening on the inside of the block.

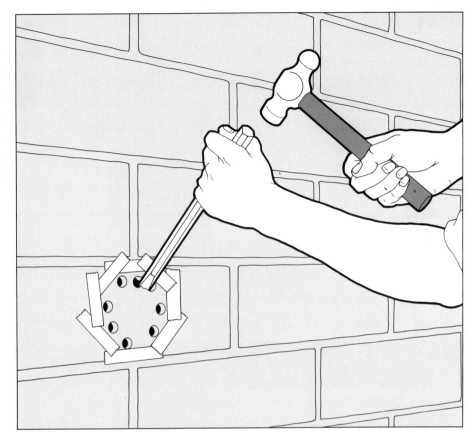

2 **Sealing the vent pipe.** Spread a 25 mm band of mortar round the exterior opening in the block. Slide the interior flange plate off the vent pipe and spread mortar round the pipe behind the hood *(right)*. Push the pipe into the opening, pressing the hood in firmly to squeeze out the excess mortar; wipe it off. Working inside the house, clean away any mortar inside the pipe. Spread mortar round the interior opening in the block, then slip the flange on to the pipe and press it on firmly. Wipe off the excess. Attach the duct to the pipe and drier *(Step 3, left)*.

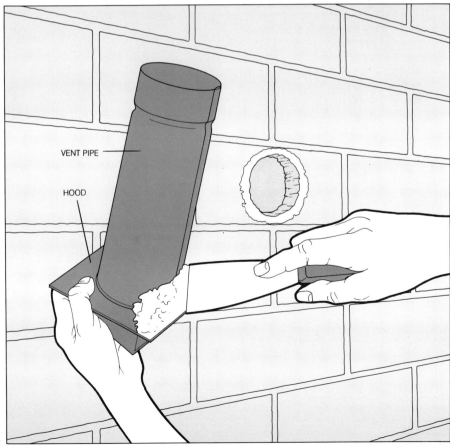

VENT PIPE

HOOD

3 Shielding against Cold and Heat

By general agreement, the great majority of houses built before 1970 are inadequately protected against winter and summer weather. These homes are poorly caulked or weatherstripped, have doors and windows that are not tight-fitting or, most important, have poor insulation in their ceilings, walls and floors. If they were effectively protected, the savings would come to nearly a fifth of the money spent on home heating and cooling every year.

Because poor insulation accounts for the greatest waste of fuel, this chapter tells how to improve the insulation you already have and how to install it in areas that have none. In each case, the object is the same: to block the flow of heat into or out of the house. Heat always flows from an area of higher temperature to one of lower, just as water flows from a high point to a lower one. Some materials are good conductors of the flow of heat—the aluminium or copper bottom of a pan, for instance, quickly passes heat from the flame below it to the food above. Others, like the fireproof mat that keeps the hot pan from scorching a work surface, resist the flow.

Wood, sheet glass, metal and solid masonry—the materials used to build a house—are generally poor resisters of heat flow. Certain natural and man-made insulating materials, however, resist it superbly. A modern glass-fibre blanket only 150 mm thick blocks the flow of heat as effectively as 2.5 metres of solid brick wall. Unfortunately, many homes do not take advantage of such powerful insulators. Older houses, built when fuel costs were comparatively low, saved on insulation but waste electricity, oil and gas. To make them economical today, they need a systematic programme of analysis and installation.

First, compare the insulation you have with the insulation you need. Next, check to see that your insulation is at the right level—first in the attic or roof, where warm rising air causes the greatest heat loss, then in exterior walls, and finally in the basement or the areas under suspended timber floors at the bottom of the house. The cost of rectifying insulation deficiencies can usually be recovered in terms of fuel savings within four years—sometimes in as little as two—and the result is a house that is not only less expensive to maintain but also more comfortable in all weathers.

Windows and doors call for a different treatment. They cannot be insulated in the usual way, but they do form paths of heat loss in winter and unwanted heat gain in summer. Double-glazed windows or doors, with a layer of insulating air trapped by a sheet of glass or plastic, cut these losses and gains by as much as half. Other alternatives include insulating shutters and heavy, lined curtains or blinds. And for the special problem of summer glare and heat, there is an old-fashioned solution with some new-fangled improvements—awnings, which are now often made of plastic or aluminium, or plastic window film that serves the same purpose.

A Guide to the Complexities of Insulation

All home insulating materials have certain features in common. Light for their bulk, they are fluffy or foamy—even rigid insulation boards have the feel of congealed foam. They have these qualities because they consist mainly of tiny pockets of trapped air.

The air pockets resist the flow of heat out of or into a house. Heating engineers rate the resistance on a scale of R-values, based on the amount of heat that will pass through a square metre of material in one hour when the temperature on one side is 1°C higher than on the other side. The R-value depends on both the composition and thickness of the material (chart, below).

By far the most common material used for insulation consists of mineral fibres—fibres of glass or of rockwool, which is made by blowing steam through molten rock. There are two common ways of packaging this material: in long rolls that are called mats, or pre-cut flexible rectangles called slabs (opposite page, top).

Mineral fibres and cellulose fibre, which is made from shredded newsprint and other papers, can also be used as loose-fill insulation, poured or blown on to attic floors or into hollow walls. Besides fibres, loose fill may consist of pellets or granules, usually made of vermiculite (a form of mica) or perlite (volcanic ash).

The remaining insulating materials are man-made synthetics. One type comes in rigid boards or sheets and is widely used to insulate masonry walls. Another type consists of a plastic foam that flows round obstructions to fill a space completely, then hardens to a rigid mass.

By blocking heat flow, insulation solves one problem but introduces another. It increases the temperature difference between inside and outside wall surfaces. And temperature determines how much vapour air can hold; moisture that is vapour at the interior temperature turns to liquid at the lower exterior temperature. The water makes insulation worthless, and damages paint and wood.

The solution to the problem is a vapour barrier—a layer of impervious material that prevents water vapour from reaching a section cold enough to make it condense. Where a vapour barrier is not incorporated as an integral part of a mat or slab, one should be installed over the insulation material. With loose fill, you can either install a separate barrier or cover the interior of an insulated wall with oil-base enamel paint and a top coat of alkyd paint.

Types of Insulation

Material	Approximate R-value per 100 mm of thickness	Form	Advantages	Disadvantages
Vermiculite	1.5	Loose fill	Especially suitable for the spaces in hollow-core blocks	Low insulation efficiency; moisture-absorbent
Perlite	2.1	Loose fill	Easily poured into hollow spaces	Comparable to vermiculite
Glass fibre	2.5	Mats, slabs, loose fill	Relatively inexpensive; non-combustible	Fibres can irritate skin
Rockwool	2.5	Mats, slabs, loose fill	Comparable to glass fibre; non-combustible	Fibres can irritate skin
Cellulose	2.6	Loose fill	Fine consistency permits loose-fill installation	Requires professional installation; inflammable unless chemically treated
Polystyrene	2.7	Rigid boards, loose fill	Moisture-resistant; useful for below-grade floors and exterior walls	Highly combustible; easily dented
Urea formaldehyde	3.3	Foamed-in-place	High insulation efficiency; good for exterior walls	Requires professional installation; not used in exposed coastal situations
Urethane	4.3	Rigid boards or foamed-in-place	Highest insulation efficiency	Foam requires professional installation; gives off noxious gases if ignited

Comparing insulation materials. Although insulation is marketed under a bewildering variety of trade names, almost all of it uses one of the basic materials listed by their generic names on this chart. Glass fibre and rockwool account for more than 80 per cent of all insulation sold for attics in the U.K., France and Germany, but the others have distinctive forms or properties, listed in the latter three columns, that make them preferable to fibres in some applications.

The materials are ranked in an ascending order of resistance to heat flow, or R-value. The rating is printed on all mats, slabs and boards. The 100 mm mineral fibre mat will be rated R-2.5, the value recommended for exterior walls in a moderate climatic area. When you buy loose fill, look for bags that indicate the R-value of the insulation at different thicknesses and densities.

How Insulation is Packaged

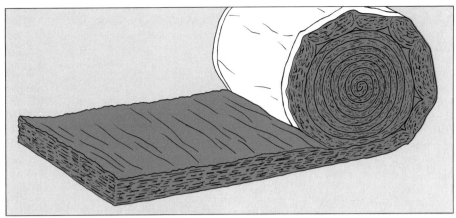

Mats. These rolls of insulation are sold in thicknesses of 80 to 160 mm, lengths of up to 9 metres, and widths of up to 1200 mm designed to fit snugly between standard stud spacings. Mats may have thin marginal strips, called flanges, for stapling. They may have a vapour barrier of polythene or foil, or a moisture barrier of paper (which does not prevent the passage of vapour); they are also available without barriers. Mats are best for long runs of unobstructed space: between floor joists in an unfinished attic or between rafters in a roof.

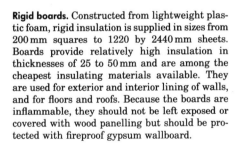

Slabs. These are simply short, stiff mats, cut into uniform lengths of 600, 900 or 1200 mm, for easier handling. Friction-fit slabs without attached vapour barriers can be squeezed between studs, joists or rafters without fasteners.

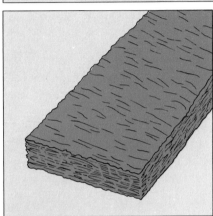

Rigid boards. Constructed from lightweight plastic foam, rigid insulation is supplied in sizes from 200 mm squares to 1220 by 2440 mm sheets. Boards provide relatively high insulation in thicknesses of 25 to 50 mm and are among the cheapest insulating materials available. They are used for exterior and interior lining of walls, and for floors and roofs. Because the boards are inflammable, they should not be left exposed or covered with wood panelling but should be protected with fireproof gypsum wallboard.

Loose fill. This type is easy to spread into open, flat spaces, such as unfloored attics. It can also be blown into cavity walls through access holes by specialist contractors. When used in attics, a separate vapour barrier must be installed. Vermiculite granules are light and easy to lay, but can be blown out of position in a draughty attic; mineral fibre and cellulose loose fill must be installed by professional contractors.

How a Vapour Barrier Works

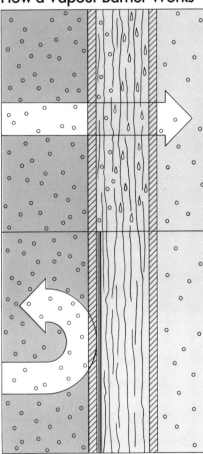

Blocking water vapour. In winter, when the interior temperature of an insulated building is much higher than that of the air outside, warm, moist interior air releases its moisture as it passes through insulation *(top)*, condensing into water inside the insulation or on the cold inner surface of the exterior wall.

A vapour barrier of aluminium foil, heavy plastic sheeting or waterproof paint *(bottom)* prevents water vapour from passing beyond the insulation's interior surface—it never reaches a cold region and cannot condense.

Where to Insulate a House

Houses are built in many shapes and sizes, but all of them incorporate some of the elements of the dwelling on the right. Using this drawing as a guide, make a check list of the walls, ceilings and floors that should be insulated in your own home to reduce heating and air-conditioning bills.

The overall rule for insulating a house is simple: insulation should be present at any surface separating living spaces from unheated areas, since that is where heat loss occurs—and also where the sun's heat can make unwelcome entry in the summer. Windows can be double-glazed. All exterior walls should, if possible, be insulated, not neglecting any wall of a split-level house that rises above an adjacent roof. Any wall between a heated room and an unheated area such as a garage, utility room or open porch also demands insulation, as do floors separating living spaces from such unheated areas. And do not overlook the overhanging portion of a room cantilevered out from the rest of the house.

If the house has an unheated cellar, the floors above must be insulated. In the case of a finished basement, the below-ground walls require insulation. Similarly, the floor of an unheated attic calls for insulation, whereas a finished room in a heated attic must have an insulated ceiling and knee walls as well as protection for the ceilings and walls of all dormers.

Where insulation goes. Because heated air rises and is lost through the roof, the most critical insulation sites in this house are the floor of the unfinished attic and the roof above the finished attic. To complete the envelope protecting the heated interior from the unheated exterior, the exterior walls should be protected. Then come the ceilings of the unheated basement. Not to be neglected are such heat escape routes as dormers and overhangs, which should also be insulated. The figures beside each arrow indicate typical heat losses in an uninsulated house as a percentage of total heat lost from the house.

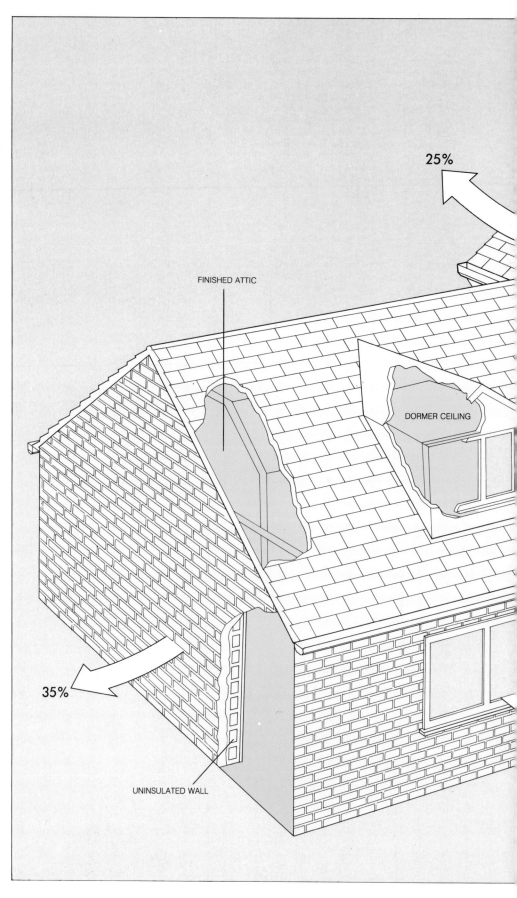

FINISHED ATTIC

25%

DORMER CEILING

35%

UNINSULATED WALL

UNFINISHED ATTIC

SINGLE-GLAZED
WINDOW

10%

15%

15%

UNHEATED BASEMENT

The Attic: Where Insulation Pays Off Most

Attic insulation is the most important in the house, not only because heat is lost up through the attic in winter, but also because attics build up heat in summer. So insulating your house begins here, whether your attic is simply an unfinished, unheated, unused space without a floor *(below)*; an unfinished and probably unheated storage area with a floor *(pages 76–77)*; or a finished room, heated and perhaps even occupied *(pages 80–81)*. And do not forget to insulate the stairway or access hatch; in most homes, this acts as a gaping hole for heat transfer. However, do not seal your attic space completely; adequate insulation must be combined with adequate ventilation *(pages 60–61)*.

The most practical insulation for the attic is mats of glass fibre or mineral wool *(pages 70–71)*. Loose fill, which is simply poured into place to the depths of the joists and levelled off with a straight piece of wood, is useful for awkward corners and between joists of uneven widths. Mats are sold in rolls which state the width and length (and sometimes the area) on the packaging. To work out how many rolls you need, calculate the area of your attic by multiplying its width and length and dividing it by the area of each roll. Remember that the rolls of mat appear compact, but they will expand more than four times

their thickness once opened; do not unwrap the rolls before you get them into the attic and unwrap only one package at a time.

If your attic is unfinished and unfloored, you will probably need to install temporary lighting and flooring. Hang one or more safety lights, set boards across several joists to hold your weight (the exposed ceiling will probably break if you step on it) and lay down other boards to support the insulation. You will need a serrated knife or handsaw to cut the mat, and a staple gun. Wear gloves, a breathing mask and goggles; a hard hat is also advisable to protect your head against protruding roofing nails under the eaves.

Mat for an Unfinished Floor

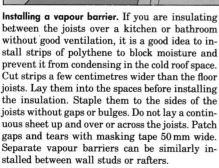

Installing a vapour barrier. If you are insulating between the joists over a kitchen or bathroom without good ventilation, it is a good idea to install strips of polythene to block moisture and prevent it from condensing in the cold roof space. Cut strips a few centimetres wider than the floor joists. Lay them into the spaces before installing the insulation. Staple them to the sides of the joists without gaps or bulges. Do not lay a continuous sheet up and over or across the joists. Patch gaps and tears with masking tape 50 mm wide. Separate vapour barriers can be similarly installed between wall studs or rafters.

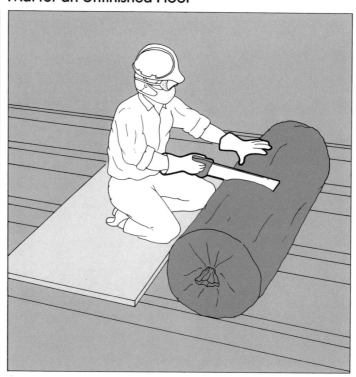

1 Cutting insulation mat. Rolls of insulation usually come in widths of 400 or 1200 mm. A standard joist width is 350 mm. To achieve a snug fit, the mat should be slightly wider than the space between the joists, so unless the joist is unusually narrow it is not worth cutting 400 mm insulation. However, if you have bought a 1200 mm wide roll or if your joists are of varying widths, you will need to cut the roll to fit. This is most easily done if the insulation is still in its package. Rest the roll across the joists with one end flush with the outside edge of one joist. Using a handsaw or serrated knife, cut the roll flush with the outside edge of the next joist.

2 **Laying mat between joists.** Unroll the mat between the joists, starting at the eaves at one end. Be careful not to jam it right into the eaves because this would block the flow of air through the attic space *(inset)*. Proprietary vents that hold the insulation away from the roof can be fitted into the eaves. Use a pole to push the mat into hard-to-reach places.

3 **Fitting mat round obstacles.** Cut the insulation to fit snugly round protruding objects. Pipes running between the joists should be covered by the insulation but electric cables should lie over it so that they do not overheat. Butt mats against each other at noggings. When chimneys are surrounded by joists and noggings, either cut mat to fit or lay loose fill in the space between.

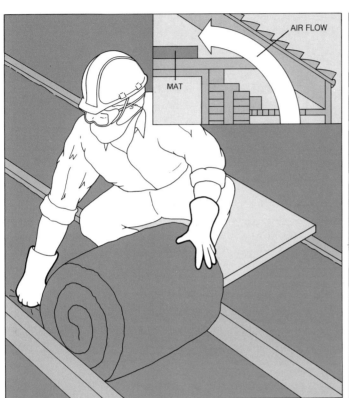

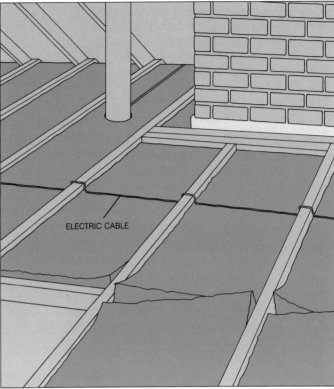

An Extra Layer For Extra Protection

Adding insulation. If your existing insulation is below the recommended thickness, it is a simple matter to add another layer of mat between the joists. If the existing layer is laid at right angles to the joists and draped over them, slit the insulation along the length of the joists *(left)* and tuck it down before adding the second layer. Laying insulation across the joists has several drawbacks: it is difficult to cover the gaps between adjacent strips and anything placed on the insulation will squash it and reduce its effectiveness. Covering the joists also makes moving around in the attic very dangerous. If you wish to use the attic for storage and have already insulated to the top of the joists, lay chipboard at least 12 mm thick, a good insulator, across the joists.

Insulating an Attic Ceiling

An unfinished attic with a floor can be insulated simply by stapling insulation mat with a vapour barrier between studs on the end walls and also between the rafters of the roof *(right)*. But it is more effective to hang insulation below the roof peak, if necessary installing "collar" ceiling beams to support friction-fit slabs. The space between the beams and the peak of the roof, when combined with the vents shown on pages 60–61, will act as a channel to remove excess heat and water vapour. The collar beams can be either 100 by 50 mm or 50 by 25 mm pieces of timber nailed across rafters, but if you use 150 by 50 mm pieces, with bevelled ends to match the slope of the roof, you will be one step closer to finishing your attic.

Warmth for a New Room

1 Installing the beams. Cut 100 by 50 mm pieces of timber to span each pair of rafters across the attic at a convenient ceiling height, making them long enough to reach the roof sheathing at both ends. Drive nails through the beams into the sides of the rafters.

Insulating without collar beams. Fit insulation mat between the rafters with the vapour barriers facing you. Leave a little air space between the insulation material and the roof for ventilation. Staple flanges to the edges of the rafters every 150 mm, and butt the mat ends at the roof peak, overlapping the flanges. Insulate end walls as in Step 3 *(opposite page)*.

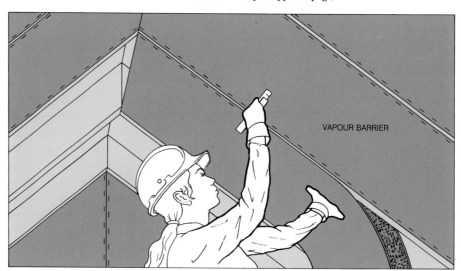

VAPOUR BARRIER

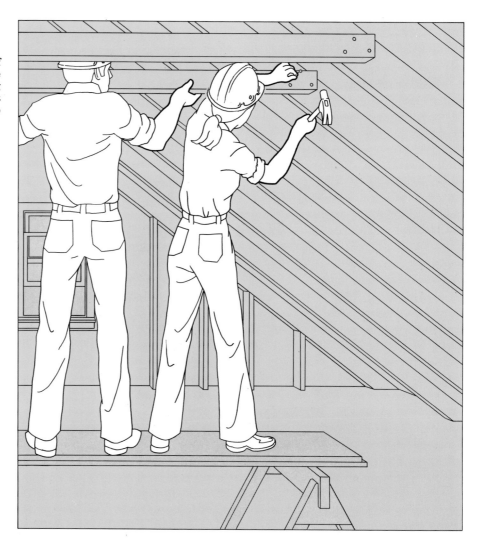

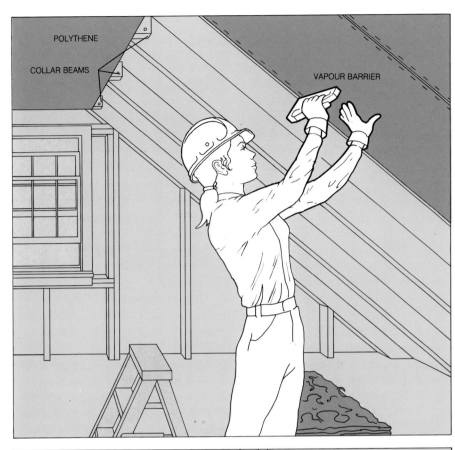

POLYTHENE

COLLAR BEAMS

VAPOUR BARRIER

2 **Installing ceiling insulation.** Squeeze friction-fit slabs between the collar beams and staple a continuous sheet of polythene over them to act as a vapour barrier. Then staple insulation mat between rafters from the collar beams down to the floor. Tape the edges of insulation where the collar beams and the rafters meet, to make a continuous vapour barrier.

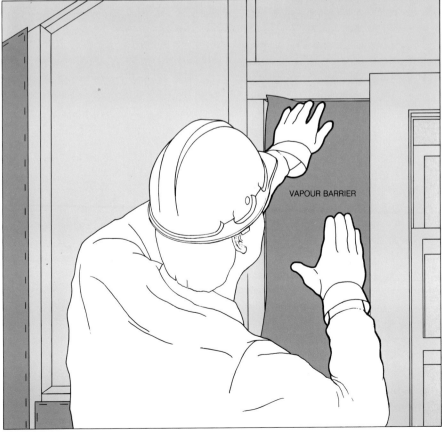

VAPOUR BARRIER

3 **Insulating the end walls.** Unless the walls are built with wooden studs, you will need to attach battens to the end walls as described on page 83. Install insulation mat between studs or battens with the vapour barrier facing you. Trim the mat to fit all angles and round windows and ventilation points such as air-bricks.

Insulating an Attic Access

Access to an unfinished attic—whether it is an open stairwell or just a hatchway—can be a major hole in the blanket of insulation, undermining the hard work you put into packing insulation between floor joists, collar beams and rafters.

If there is a stairway, make sure it has a door, glue a rigid insulation board to the back and draught-strip round the doorway. Hatchways may be treated in the same way as doors, or fitted with a leftover piece of fibre insulation *(right)*. A hatchway with a ladder attached presents more of a challenge. The best way to seal cracks round the opening is to build an insulated box in the attic that encloses it as well as the ladder. The top of the box is provided with a hinged lid you push up as you climb.

Insulating a hatchway. Cut a 100 mm thick piece of fibre insulation to fit the top of the hatch door and secure it with 50 mm wide hessian tape nailed to the sides with broad-headed nails *(below)*. Alternatively, you can tie the insulation down with string looped round nails driven into the sides. Clean the ledge on which the door sits and fit it with a plastic V-shaped draught-strip, which will be compressed by the weight of the door when the hatch is closed.

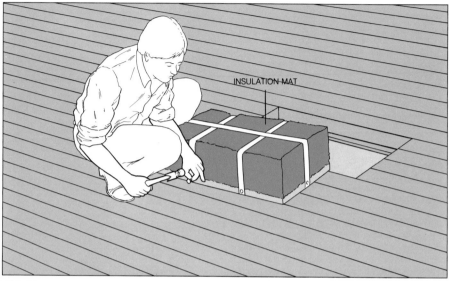

INSULATION MAT

A Box for a Hatchway

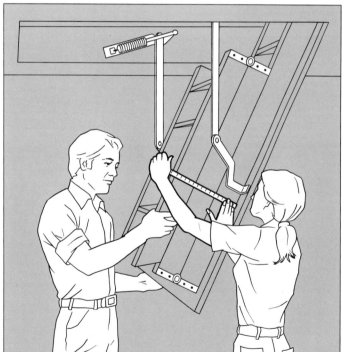

1 Measuring the stairway depth. If the hatchway contains pull-down steps, lower them but do not unfold the folding type. Measure the thickness to determine how much clearance the stairs need when they are raised into the attic.

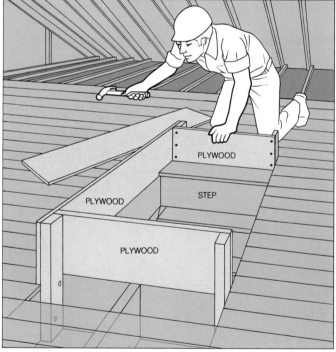

PLYWOOD

PLYWOOD

STEP

PLYWOOD

2 Building the box frame. Remove flooring and insulation from around the stair opening. Saw four 100 by 50 mm pieces of timber long enough to rise above the floor joists 50 mm more than the measurement made in Step 1. Nail an upright to each joist behind the corners at the ends of the hatchway. At the top of the stairs, place the uprights 250 mm back from the opening, to provide a step. Then nail 18 mm plywood to the uprights. Replace any removed flooring.

3 **Finishing the box.** Cut two lengths of 100 by 50 mm timber to match the height of the plywood; nail them through the plywood into the uprights at two corners of the box on the side where the hatchway lid will be attached. Then nail to each upright another 100 by 50 mm piece that projects 200 mm higher, so that the lid can rest against them when it is open.

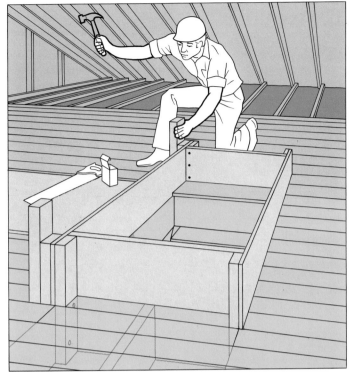

4 **Covering the frame.** Saw a lid from 9 mm plywood, big enough to extend to the outer edges of the four original uprights. To prevent warping, put a 100 by 50 mm piece of timber down one long edge of the lid, nailing through the plywood into the timber. Attach the other side of the lid with bolt-held hinges to the outside of the frame on the side of the box with the uprights *(Step 2)*. Attach a door handle to the inside of the lid at a convenient point for pulling the lid down.

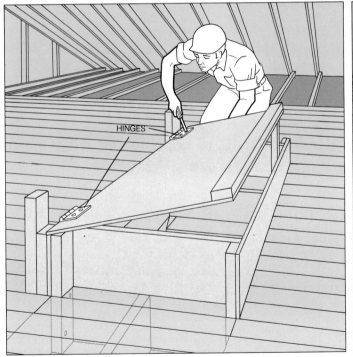

HINGES

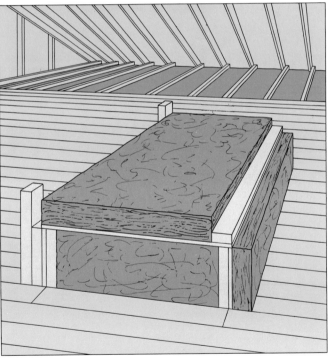

5 **Insulating the box.** Cut two pieces of insulation mat slightly longer than the short sides of the box and compress them snugly between the end uprights. Trim two more lengths of mat to fit the long sides of the box and staple their flanges to the sides. Place another length of mat on top of the lid and staple the flanges to the lid.

Insulating a Finished Attic

A finished attic is no more complicated to insulate than an unfinished one, except for cutting out passageways in the ceiling and side—or knee—walls.

Once you have got through the knee walls to the outer attic floor, insulate as shown on pages 74–75. Friction-fit slabs are installed behind knee walls and insulation mat, with its vapour barrier towards the room, on top of the level ceiling. For the sloping section of a ceiling, friction-fit slabs can be pushed down between the rafters; strips of heavy polythene slightly wider than the width of the joists should be pushed down first to act as a vapour barrier. Leave an air gap of at least 40 to 50 mm between the slabs and the underside of the roof to allow for ventilation. If the space above the ceiling is too small to manoeuvre in, insert the slabs from behind the knee wall and get a professional to blow in loose fibre above the flat section.

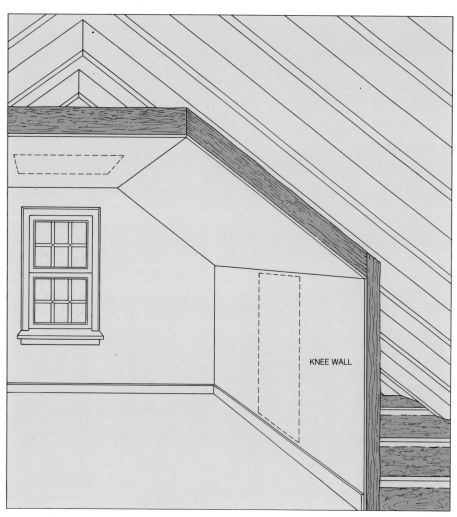

A well-insulated attic room. Mat should be installed above the flat attic ceiling and between the joists of the attic floor beyond the knee walls. Friction-fit slabs—designed to be installed without stapling flanges—should be squeezed between the studs of the knee walls. Then a polythene vapour barrier and slabs can be pushed down the sloping ceiling. Unless there are passageways to the outer attic, cut access panels *(dotted lines)* on the ceiling and knee walls.

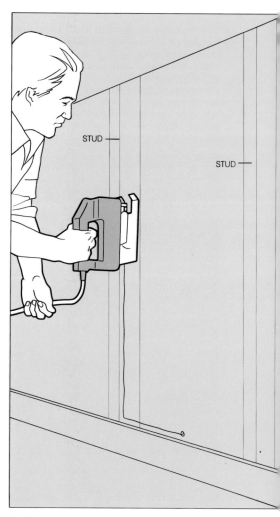

1 **Cutting an opening.** Drill a 10 mm hole through the ceiling or at the bottom of the knee wall. If there is a wall switch, do not cut near it. Cut across to the nearest joist or stud, then cut alongside it to the top or bottom. Cut across to the next joist and finish the rectangle. Remove the section of wallboard and staple a piece of mat to its back, with the vapour barrier positioned so that it faces towards the room.

2 **Insulating the walls and outer floor.** Fit mat between the joists of the outer attic floor. Staple a polythene vapour barrier to the sides of the wall studs to form a U-shape. Fit unfaced friction-fit slabs snugly between the studs. Make sure that there is a gap of at least 40 to 50 mm between the top of the slabs and the roof to allow air to circulate. If the slabs do not stay in place, tack pieces of string or wooden battens across the studs about 30 cm from the top and bottom of the slabs to hold them in place.

3 **Repairing the access opening.** Working from behind the access opening, skew-nail a 100 by 50 mm piece of wood across one end of the opening, half above and half below the cut edge. Then nail 50 by 25 mm strips of wood down the length of each joist or stud on the inside passageway edge of the access hole. Align the strips with the 100 by 50 mm piece to provide a backstop for the panel when it is replaced.

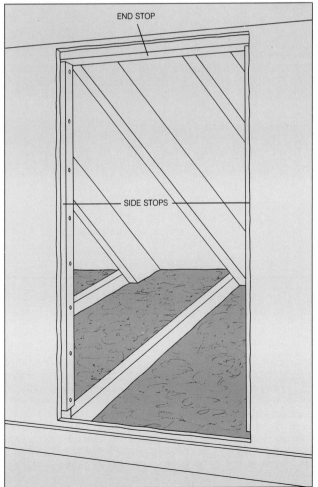

4 **Installing a replacement panel.** Working from the finished attic side, set the panel in the wallboard opening against the three strips of wood and nail it in place. Cover the joint with joint tape and spread a thin coat of joint filler over the tape with a taping knife as shown above. When the joint filler dries, put on a second layer. Sand the dry filler with fine-grade sandpaper.

Insulating Exterior Walls

While the attic needs insulation more than any other part of the house, exterior walls are next in importance. The kind of insulation you use and where you install it depends on how your wall is constructed and whether you prefer to work on the inside or outside of the house.

Most houses in this country have either solid walls two bricks thick or cavity walls with an air space between two layers of masonry. Cavity walls can be insulated by installing insulation in the cavity during construction; the job can also be done later by drilling holes in the wall from outside and injecting loose insulation, but this requires a professional installer.

Most houses built before the 1920s are of solid wall construction. They can be insulated by adding a layer of insulation and a waterproof cladding such as timber weatherboarding or plastic shiplap to the outside of the house *(pages 38–39)*, but an easier and cheaper alternative is to put insulation on the inside surfaces of the walls.

If the wall is sound and fairly even, a special insulation board incorporating a vapour barrier and a plasterboard facing can be fixed to the wall with adhesive. An alternative method is to construct a batten framework on the wall, insert mineral fibre mat or slabs or polystyrene sheets, and then cover the framework with plasterboard or another type of wallboard.

The major drawback to lining a wall inside is that living space must be sacrificed: a framework providing room for 100 mm of insulation will use up a third of a cubic metre for every 3 square metres of wall thickened. The loss can be minimized by insulating only the wall that faces away from the sun and either the west or east wall, whichever faces the prevailing winds in your area. The wall that is warmed by the sun for most of the day needs insulation only in the harshest of climates. You will also save space if you strip the plaster from the wall before fixing the battens; you may have to do this anyway if the plaster is loose or uneven.

Obstructions will have to be removed or worked around. Electrical fixtures can be brought forward to the level of the new wall surface; if there is not enough slack in the cable, however, you will need the services of an electrician. Heavy fittings such

as metal wall lamps should be relocated so that they can be screwed on to the battens. Remove skirting boards and picture rails before you start work. Door and window architraves should be framed with planed timber cut to the thickness of the insulation and wallboard combined; if you decide to restore the original appearance of the room by repositioning the architraves, they can be removed and then refixed over battens cut to the thickness of the lining.

A good vapour barrier is essential for an insulated wall—otherwise water vapour from the room will pass through the insulation and condense on the cold inside face of the wall, rotting the timber battens and

ruining the new insulation. Use an insulation mat backed with a vapour barrier or spread a continuous sheet of 500-gauge polythene sheeting over the insulation. For making the framework of battens, you should buy timber that has been pretreated, preferably by pressure-impregnation, with a preservative.

The insulation should not be less than 50 mm thick. A thickness of 75 mm to 100 mm would be better, for which you will need 75 by 50 mm or 100 by 50 mm timber battens. When buying timber, check that its actual thickness—that is, the thickness after the battens have been planed—will not be less than the thickness of the insulation.

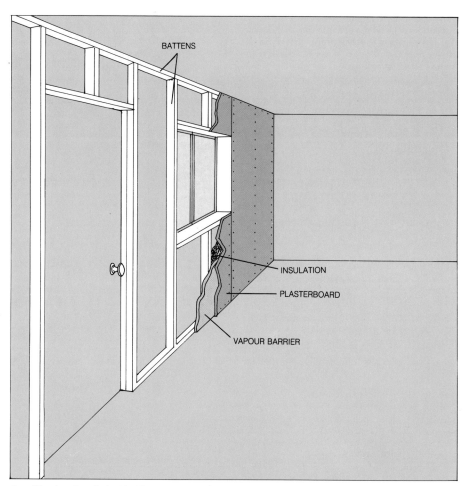

A wall insulated on the inside. This cutaway shows an inner frame, consisting of vertical battens and top and bottom horizontal battens, which thickens an exterior wall to provide space for 100 mm of mineral fibre insulation fixed between the battens. The door frame and window reveal are also framed with battens. The battens and insulation material are covered with a continuous sheet of polythene to act as a vapour barrier and the wall is finished with plasterboard.

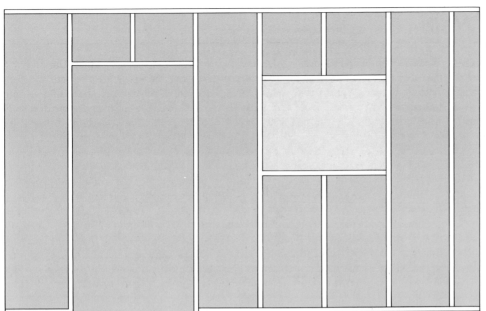

Installing the Insulation

1 A plan for framing the wall. Before starting work, measure the length and height of the wall to be insulated together with the dimensions of any door or window openings. Draw a scale plan of the wall on a piece of graph paper and mark on the plan where you will position the battens and wall boards. Horizontal battens should run along the length of the floor and ceiling. Vertical battens should be spaced with their centres no more than 600 mm apart and positioned so that the edges of the wallboards coincide with the centres of the battens. An ideal arrangement is shown on the left: the battens, with their centres 600 mm apart, support 570 mm wide rolls of insulation mat and standard-sized 1200 mm wide board. Cross battens are fitted along the top and bottom of the window opening and above the door, and are nailed to the upright battens.

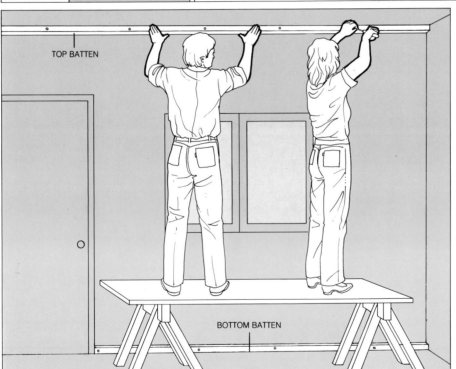

TOP BATTEN

BOTTOM BATTEN

END BATTEN

2 Fixing the top and bottom battens. Cut two pieces of timber the length of the wall. Make two saw cuts in the bottom batten to remove the doorway section. With a helper, hold the bottom batten against the wall, place a spirit level on it to make sure it is horizontal and mark the upper line of the batten on the wall. Drill holes in the batten at 600 mm intervals, then drill and plug the corresponding holes in the wall and screw the batten into position. Fix the top batten in the same way *(above)*. If the wall is uneven, the battens may need to be packed out in places with small pieces of timber known as "shims".

3 Aligning the end battens. Most corners are uneven and the two end vertical battens may need to be trimmed so that they hang in a plumb line. Hold the batten against the corner and align it with a spirit level. Get a helper to draw a line parallel to the wall down the face of the batten, using the technique described on page 93. Plane down to the line marked on the batten and hold it against the wall with the spirit level to make sure it is now plumb. Drill holes for screws and plugs and secure the battens to the wall. If the corner is badly out of square, you will need to trim the insulation to fit tightly between the battens.

4 **Fixing vertical battens.** Align remaining vertical battens using a spirit level held upright. Drill through battens at 600 mm intervals, drill and plug holes in the wall and secure battens with screws. If walls are uneven, first insert shims behind the battens. Screw cross battens to wall above and below windows and above doors. Nail cross battens to upright battens on either side.

5 **Stapling the insulation.** Using a large serrated knife, cut mineral fibre insulation to fit. Place it between the battens, keeping the vapour barrier, if one is incorporated, towards you. Staple the flanges of the mat to the battens every 150 mm with a staple gun. Scraps of mat can be butted together to fill spaces round doors and windows.

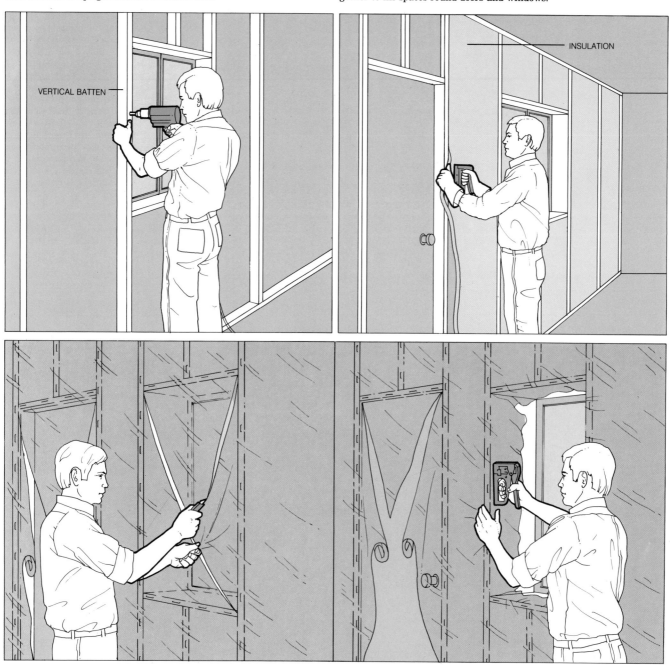

VERTICAL BATTEN

INSULATION

6 **Adding a vapour barrier.** Fasten a single piece of 500-gauge polythene over the new insulation, stapling every 150 mm along the battens. If you have to use two sheets of polythene, double-fold the two sheets together over a batten and staple them securely. Try not to make any holes in the polythene. If you rip it, seal the gap with weatherproof tape. Tape all joints and places where the polythene meets obstacles, such as electrical sockets. At every window and door, slash the plastic diagonally from corner to corner *(above, left)*. Fold each triangle into the opening; staple it to the battens *(above, right)*. Trim the triangles and seal the edges with tape.

7 Fixing the boards. Cut the boards 25 mm shorter than the floor to ceiling height and cut out holes for obstacles such as electrical sockets. Start at one corner, pressing the first board tightly against the ceiling; nail the board to the battens every 150 mm. The nails should not be closer than 13 mm from the edge of the board. Butt each board tightly against the neighbouring one.

8 Trimming window reveals. A window sill can be removed and replaced with a piece of stair-tread timber—with one rounded edge—cut 10 mm wider than the depth of the reveal and nailed in place. Or, you can leave the sill in place and fill the edge out with a piece of timber before covering it with a new sill. Cut small pieces of wallboard to fit round sides and top of reveal.

PLASTERBOARD

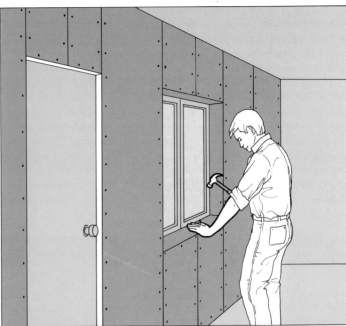

9 Creating a smooth finish. Cover the joints between wallboards with joint filler. Press joint tape into the filler and follow immediately with another coat of joint filler *(right)*. When the filler has set, apply a thin layer of joint finish over the joint, feathering out the edges. External angles round window or door reveals can be covered with a special plasterboard corner tape. Cover nail heads in the boards with joint filler to fill out the slight depressions. Paint the surface of the board with wallboard primer before decorating with paint or paper.

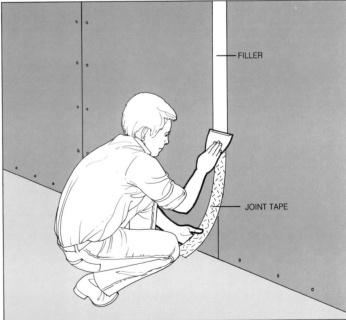

FILLER

JOINT TAPE

Completing the Job: Floors, Tanks and Pipes

Because warm air rises, some home owners assume that a well-insulated attic is all they need. But an uninsulated basement or suspended timber floor is an expensive nuisance. If a basement is heated, it needs insulation as much as any outside room. If it is both unheated and uninsulated, it will make the floors above it cold, wasting fuel and causing chills.

The worst offenders are spaces with dirt floors. Cover such floors with thick plastic sheeting. Then, if the space is unheated, install vents in the walls *(page 65)* to prevent condensation on basement beams and ground-floor walls. Finally, apply the insulation material itself.

In a heated basement, lay the insulation against the walls *(pages 88–89)*. In an un-heated space, insert mineral fibre mat, vapour-barrier side up, between the joists supporting the floor above. The mat is held in place with wire braces *(below)* or plastic netting stapled to the joists.

If you cannot get to the space under the floor, you can lift the floorboards and install the insulation from above, draping the mat over plastic netting laid between the joists. Alternatively, lay insulation on top of the floor; apply slabs of polystyrene and cover them with flooring-grade chipboard. A vapour barrier between the two layers will prevent condensation occurring on the lower surface of polystyrene.

Solid concrete ground floors with no space underneath are much better at retaining heat than suspended timber floors, but it is still worthwhile to insulate them with layers of polystyrene slab and chipboard with a vapour barrier in between as described above.

In cold climates, water pipes and cisterns in any unheated part of the house will need insulation to prevent supply lines from freezing and to conserve heat in hot-water lines. Use pre-formed mineral wool or foam cylindrical pipe sleeves, sold in a wide range of diameters. Or you can use special mineral fibre or felt pipe insulation, available in narrow strips which you spiral round the pipe. You can also use strips of insulation off-cuts fixed in the same way. To protect the insulation against moisture you should cover it with polythene sheeting taped or wired round the pipe.

Insulating the Unheated Spaces

Working with mat and braces. Push a length of insulation mat, vapour-barrier side up, into the spaces between the floor joists overhead. The barrier should just touch the sub-flooring. Every 500 mm or so install wire braces—cut from wire clothes hangers a bit longer than joist spacing—so that they barely touch the mat; crushing insulation reduces its effectiveness.

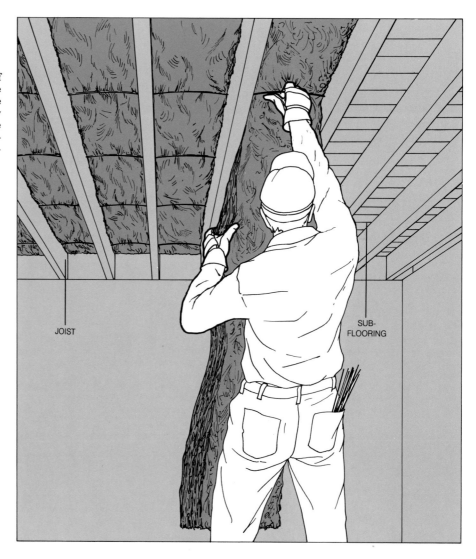

JOIST

SUB-FLOORING

Insulating a Hot Water Cylinder

Fitting a jacket. An insulating jacket at least 80 mm thick round your hot water cylinder can cut heat loss by 75 per cent. They come ready-made in a variety of sizes. Make sure there are no gaps between segments which could let the heat escape. Fasten the straps lightly round the jacket so that the insulation material is not compressed.

Sleeves for Piping

1 **A close-fitting sleeve.** Clean the pipes and scrape off rust. Cover the pipes with lengths of cylindrical pipe insulation and butt joints tightly. To make short sections of insulation, cut the sleeve with a utility knife or a handsaw.

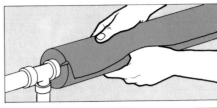

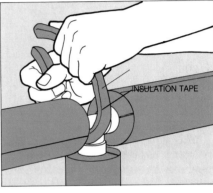

2 **Taping the fittings.** Cover the pipe fittings with insulation tape 5 mm thick. Be sure to cover the fittings completely: no part should be exposed. To complete the job, if using unfaced mineral wool sections, wrap the pipe fittings in polythene.

Lagging a Cold Water Cistern

Cutting mat to fit. Insulate the cistern while you are insulating the attic, using leftover pieces of mineral fibre mat. Wrap the insulation round the sides and secure it with string. Make a hardboard or polythene board lid to fit over the cistern, cutting it to allow water issuing from the overflow pipe to enter the cistern. Tie or glue insulation mat to the top of the hardboard and cover the whole lid with polythene to prevent stray pieces of insulation from falling in to the water. As a precaution against the water in the cistern freezing, do not lay insulation mat between the joists directly beneath the cold water cistern: some warm air should rise from below.

Insulating Heated Basements

A heated, unplastered basement or cellar, essentially part of the living area of the house, must be insulated with compact materials in a simple but effective manner to avoid considerable heat losses and allow for easy finishing of the walls. This is true whether the walls are of a single leaf or cavity wall structure.

A material commonly used for this is extruded polystyrene board. It is glued between battens to which plasterboard is nailed. The fire-resistant plasterboard protects the inflammable insulation material.

The battens should be fixed at intervals appropriate to the width of the plasterboard. For instance, 50 by 25 mm battens placed at 600 mm centres will allow for the fixing of standard 600 or 1200 mm wide plasterboard sheets.

Alternative materials for insulating walls of a heated basement are rock or glass-fibre slabs. These are fitted between upright battens; one edge of the slab is pushed against the inside of a batten and cut by drawing a sharp knife through the slab where it overlaps the next batten. The material must be tightly butted where there are joins. When the slabs are in position, install a vapour barrier *(page 84)* before nailing on the plasterboard.

The join between the wallboard and the floor can be neatly finished by covering it with a standard size skirting board. Place the board along the baseline of the wall and nail it to the horizontal base batten and the uprights.

1 Attaching the battens. Fix horizontal 50 mm by 25 mm battens along the top and bottom of the walls, using either drive nails or screws and plugs every 600 mm. Frame any windows in the same way. Then fix upright battens in all corners and along the walls, with their centres 600 mm apart. Finally, fix horizontal battens to create a grid pattern to fit the panels of extruded polystyrene insulation board—usually 600 by 300 mm. Use a spirit level and plumb bob line to check the horizontal and vertical alignment of the strips.

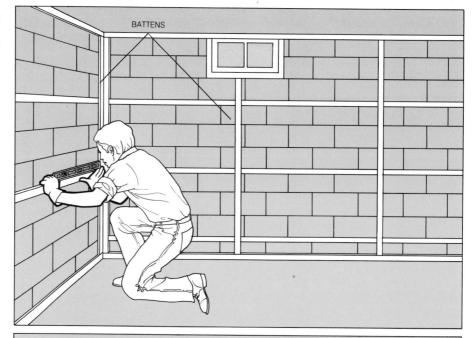

BATTENS

2 Fitting the rigid insulation. Apply construction adhesive to the backs of the insulation boards in the amount and pattern specified by the manufacturer—a common pattern is shown on the right. Mount the insulation on the wall between the battens, cutting the boards to size with a utility knife or a handsaw. The boards must fill the spaces between strips snugly.

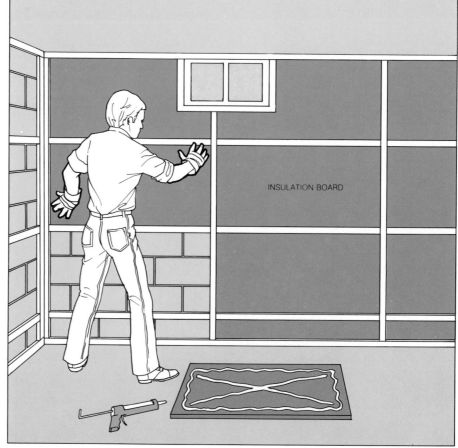

INSULATION BOARD

3 **Covering the insulation.** For fire protection, nail to the battens 12.5 mm thick panels of plasterboard. The plasterboard should be used even if you plan to cover it with modern panelling. When attaching the plasterboard, support the bottom edges temporarily on scraps of battens. When you pull the scraps from under the panels, the 25 mm space left will protect the wall from any moisture that accumulates on the floor.

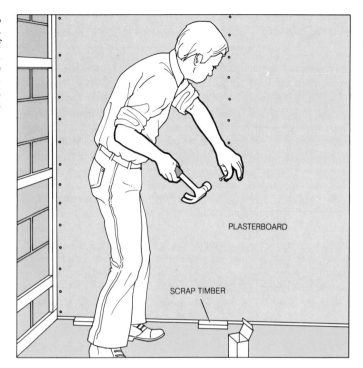

PLASTERBOARD

SCRAP TIMBER

Insulating Outer Joists and Headers

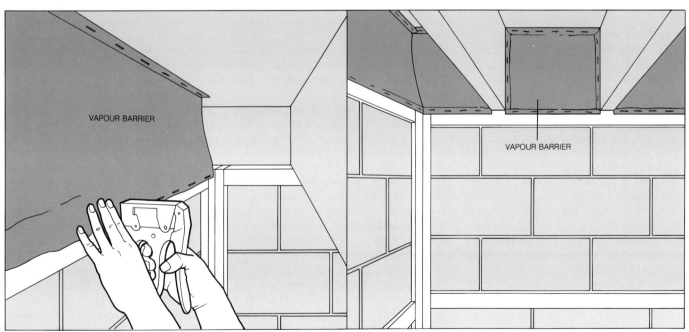

VAPOUR BARRIER

VAPOUR BARRIER

Fitting insulation mat. If the basement is under a suspended timber floor, the outer joists and headers—the spaces enclosed by the ends of joists, the top of the wall and the subflooring—should also be insulated. For the joists, use strips of flanged insulation mat *(above, left)*. Install the mat with vapour barrier facing you and insulation tucked into the contours of the space; staple one flange to the subflooring and the other to the top of the batten frame. Insulate the headers with sections of mat, cut with a 25 mm overlap at top and bottom *(above, right)*. Fit the sections between joists. Staple existing flanges to joist sides, then push back the insulation at top and bottom to form flanges and staple these to the subflooring and batten framework.

Insulating Windows

Windows are notorious energy wasters. During the winter they let precious heat escape, sending fuel bills soaring. In the summer they allow sunlight into a room, overheating it and perhaps driving up air-conditioning costs.

Windows act as heat conductors partly because glass is a rather poor insulator. Mostly, however, heat is lost because the glass used in windows is so thin—usually about 4 mm, as compared with the 225 mm or 275 mm breadth of typical brick walls. The rate at which heat flows through a particular material is usually expressed as a U-value—a figure, determined by experiment, that measures the number of watts that will pass through one metre of the material when the air temperature on one side is 1°C higher than on the other. A single-glazed window 3 to 4 mm thick has a U-value of 5.6 or even higher; a solid brick 225 mm wall has one of only 2.15, indicating a heat loss of less than half.

Fortunately, keeping outside heat from coming in through a window is easy, because much of it enters in the form of sunlight. You need only cover the window or shield it from the sun—a task efficiently performed by a variety of shades, blinds, shutters and awnings *(pages 103–111)*.

Preventing heat from passing out through windows is more difficult, in part because heat exits not only through the glass, but also through cracks around the frame. Caulking and weatherstripping window frames *(pages 8–11)* will dramatically reduce the outflow of heat. But the most effective solution in the long run is to insulate the window glass itself by adding extra layers of glazing that may be either permanent or seasonal, and covering them on cold nights with additional insulating shutters or shades.

A second layer of glazing can reduce heat loss by almost half by creating an insulating pocket of trapped air between the two panes. The panes should be at least 12 mm, but not more than 25 mm, apart to achieve the optimum effect. A further heat saving of up to one third can be achieved by adding a third layer of glazing.

One of the most common methods of multiple-glazing consists of installing interior secondary windows fitted with single or double panes of glass *(pages 92–99)*. You can buy factory-made secondary windows or else make your own, either by using plastic or aluminium units available in kits or—if you are a competent woodworker—by cutting wooden frames.

A less expensive and equally effective technique is to fashion interior windows of rigid plastic or plastic film. The plastic is either mounted on frames (available in kits) or secured directly to the window casing with screws, magnetic tape or double-sided adhesive tape *(page 102)*.

A third technique is to replace individual window panes with sealed double-glazed units, sometimes known as insulating glass *(page 100)*. Although relatively expensive, these units are unobtrusive, and they enable windows to be opened and closed in the normal way. If your existing window frames cannot be altered or reconstructed to accommodate the thicker panes, the entire window can be replaced with a prefabricated model with double or triple glazing—a job which is best left to a professional installer.

When adding multiple glazing, remember that the windows facing the sun serve as heat collectors during cold weather, transmitting warming, energy-saving sunshine into the house. A second layer of glazing added to these windows should be made of one of the high-transmission materials listed in the chart on the opposite page, such as acrylic or treated polyester. Ordinary window glass is transparent, but it has a shiny surface that allows sunlight to bounce off it. The duller, high-transmission glazing materials absorb most of the sun's rays, allowing more heat to pass through them.

Usually it is not worthwhile to triple-glaze windows facing the sun. Whatever the material used, a third layer will reduce the passage of light, and the resulting loss of solar heat in cold climates may actually offset the heat-retaining value of the additional insulation.

To reduce heat loss further, windows may be blacked out completely at night with any variety of opaque insulating materials. Lightweight insulating fabric, available at many furnishing fabric shops, can raise the insulating value of a single-glazed window substantially; on a multi-glazed window, the extra insulation can reduce the total U-value close to that of the surrounding walls. Covered with decorative furnishing fabric, the insulating material can be fashioned into a variety of heat-saving window coverings—one example is the concertina-pleated Roman blind shown on pages 103–105, which can be attached to a metal window frame with flexible magnetic strips.

Interior shutters of rigid foam insulation are an inexpensive alternative to bulky fabric window coverings. Pop-in shutters made of ordinary polystyrene foam board—similar to the material used for picnic coolers—are easy to construct and at a thickness of only 25 mm will reduce a window's U-value to 0.9. But they also have drawbacks. They must be removed from the window and stored during the day; they tend to shrink or warp with age; and unless they are coated with a fire-retarding paint, they may burn or give off toxic fumes when exposed to flame.

Hinged bifold shutters *(pages 106–107)*, faced with fire-resistant fabric or a thin skin of wood or plastic, take longer to construct, but once installed they are sturdier, less hazardous and far more convenient.

Multiple-glazing can improve problems of condensation, although it will not cure them. Condensation may form on the inner surfaces of a secondary glazed window, particularly if there is a poor seal between the secondary frame and the supporting frame. Install any multiple-glazing on a cold, dry day when the moisture content of the air is at its lowest.

The Basic Glazing Materials

Material	Form	Characteristics
Window glass	Rigid single sheets 3 to 10 mm thick; the thickness used depends upon the area being glazed. Hermetically sealed double-wall sheets 12 to 20 mm thick are available in standard window sizes. Both types are available in clear, anti-sun and obscured sheets.	Most durable and readily available glazing material. Heavier and requires stronger framing than plastics.
Acrylic	Rigid single sheets 1.5 to 10 mm thick, double-wall sheets commonly 3 mm thick. Sold in sheets of up to 3 by 2 metres. Available in patterned sheets or thermoformed panels. Tinted or clear.	Excellent light transmission, durability and light weight make it a good—but expensive—glazing material. Tougher than glass but scratches easily.
Polycarbonate	Rigid single or double-wall sheets 1 to 12 mm thick but commonly 3 to 6 mm thick; similar in appearance to acrylic and cut in the same manner.	More resistant to impact and high temperature than acrylic. Semi-transparent double-wall sheets are virtually indestructible, thus useful for home security.
Fibreglass reinforced polyester (FRP)	Flexible sheets, can be cut to any length or width; also available in more rigid multiple-layer sheets. Not as common as acrylic and polycarbonate.	Translucent but not transparent. Strong, light and inexpensive.
Polyvinyl chloride (PVC)	Flexible sheets in common thicknesses of 0.25, 0.5 and 0.8 mm. Available in rolls wide enough to span most windows.	Not as durable as the plastics above and also less clear. Scratches easily but is quite tough.
Polyester	Film, commonly 0.125 or 0.175 mm thick in rolls 650 to 1500 mm wide. Available in a variety of tints or coated with metallic, reflective surfaces.	Inexpensive, high-transmission material for interior use when treated with ultraviolet stabilizers; untreated film deteriorates quickly. Wrinkles and tears easily.
Polythene	Film, usually manufactured in the thickness of 4 or 6 mm; available in rolls usually 300 or 450 mm wide, up to 50 metres long.	Least expensive, but degrades rapidly and melts in moderate heat. Wrinkles and tears easily. Adequate for temporary use.

Choosing a glazing. This chart lists the glazings best suited to insulating windows—from traditional glass to film as thin as that used for a plastic sandwich bag. All of the glazing materials are either transparent or translucent, and many of them are available in a variety of tints or with decorative finishes and coatings. Some of the rigid glazing materials are available in what is known as double-wall form: prefabricated double-glazed sheets, with two separate layers that are connected and held parallel by sealed edges or interior connectors.

Multiple-Pane Windows for Comfort and Convenience

Adding layers of glass and plastic. Three techniques for adding layers of glazing are illustrated here, as seen from the inside of a single casement window. True double glazing *(below, left; pages 100–101),* the most effective and expensive of the methods, involves replacing single-pane glass with hermetically sealed insulating glass—two 6 mm panes separated by an airspace and sealed round the edges. Secondary glazing *(below, centre; pages 98–99)* consists of a single or double window pane that is attached to the inside of an existing window. If the system is properly installed, it can be attractive, durable and efficient, although it is unlikely to be as unobtrusive and efficient as double glazing. Some systems allow for the glass or plastic panes to be replaced with a screen or solar plastic film in the summer.

Thin plastic film *(below, right; page 102)* inside the window is an inexpensive alternative or addition to any of the other installations and works equally well. It is easy to install—it can be stuck to the window frame with double-sided adhesive tape—but it is not durable and it will have to be replaced each year.

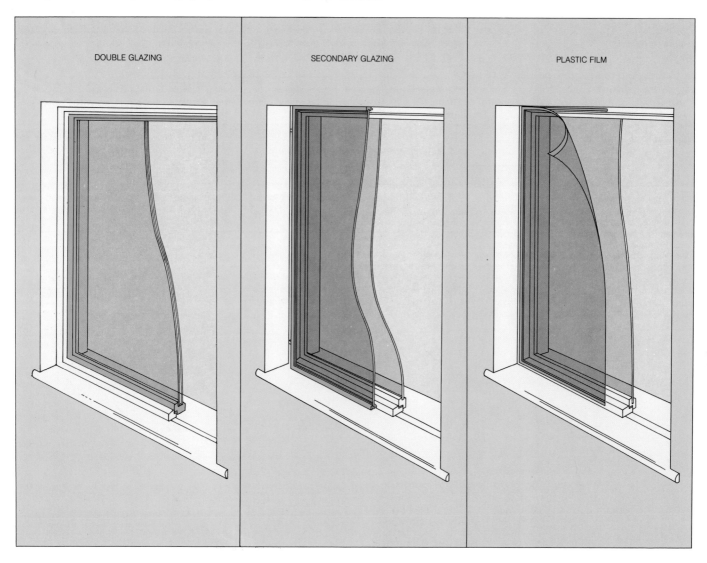

DOUBLE GLAZING

SECONDARY GLAZING

PLASTIC FILM

Making a Secondary Window Frame

Kits for making secondary windows with plastic or aluminium frames are widely available and easy to install *(pages 98–99 and 102)*. Fitted inside existing windows, however, the appearance of these frames may not always match the original windows or decor. Home-made wooden frames take more time to construct, but they will complement the wooden casements that are found in most houses, and wood is a better insulating material than either plastic or aluminium.

Double windows should be insulated with matching secondary windows hinged at either side of the casement with a meeting rebate at the centre. Small or narrow single windows can be insulated with a single framed pane; because glass and wood are both heavy materials, however, you should construct double secondary windows for large single windows, or use aluminium for the inner frame.

The double secondary window shown below and on the following pages is constructed in three stages. First, a subframe made from 50 by 25 mm hardwood is fitted in the reveal against the existing window to provide square anchorage for the secondary window. Then the two inner frames which will hold the glass are made by gluing and screwing together double thicknesses of plywood so as to form a frame front and a frame back. By using three different widths of plywood for the frames of the secondary window, a glazing channel is created all round the inside edge and a meeting rebate along one edge of each frame. Finally, the secondary frames are glazed and fixed to the subframe with surface-mounted cranked hinges, designed for use on plywood.

The tools you will need for the job are a saw, a spirit level, a steel square and a drill with a countersinking bit. You will also need woodworking glue, glazing pins and putty. A good workbench for cutting the wood is essential.

Measure the distance between the edge of the reveal and the edge of the existing windowframe: the combined width of the new subframe and inner plywood frame should not overlap the sightline of the existing window. Always check the measurement before cutting a piece of wood.

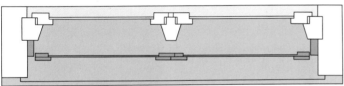

The finished installation. A secondary window fitted inside an existing window creates an air gap which reduces the amount of heat lost through the window. The cross-section above illustrates how the two wooden inner frames of the secondary window are hinged to a subframe, which is screwed directly into the reveal.

1 **Fitting the sides of the subframe.** Cut two pieces of hardwood the full length of the window reveal. Hold one piece in position against the window with its wide face towards the reveal and level it with a spirit level. If there are any gaps between the vertical hardwood and the reveal, rest a pencil tip against a small object the width of the widest gap and draw a line down the edge of the wood parallel to the wall *(right)*. Plane the wood down to the line until the piece fits against the wall with the outer edge plumb. Fit the other piece of hardwood to the opposite side of the reveal in the same way.

SUBFRAME SIDE

2 **Securing the subframe sides.** Drill pilot holes every 200 mm or so down the centre of the two sides of the subframe; avoid the areas where hinges will be fitted *(Step 7, page 96)*. Bevel the holes with a countersink bit so that they can be filled and painted later. Screw the two frame sides into position in the window reveal.

3 **Completing the subframe.** Measure the width between the two upright sections of the subframe: it should be the same distance top and bottom. Cut two pieces of hardwood to this width and fit them in the same way as the vertical sections.

4 **Laying out the front of the inner frames.** Cut four pieces of 50 mm wide plywood to fit lengthwise inside the subframe. Then measure the width inside the subframe, halve the figure, deduct 100 mm, then cut four pieces of 50 mm plywood to the resulting figure. Take two of the long pieces and two of the short and lay them out following the arrangement shown on the right. Repeat with the remaining four pieces. For a single window, cut only two length pieces and two width pieces; cut the width pieces 100 mm shorter than the width inside the subframe.

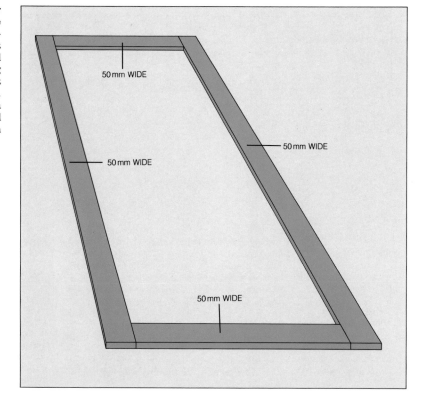

50 mm WIDE

50 mm WIDE

50 mm WIDE

50 mm WIDE

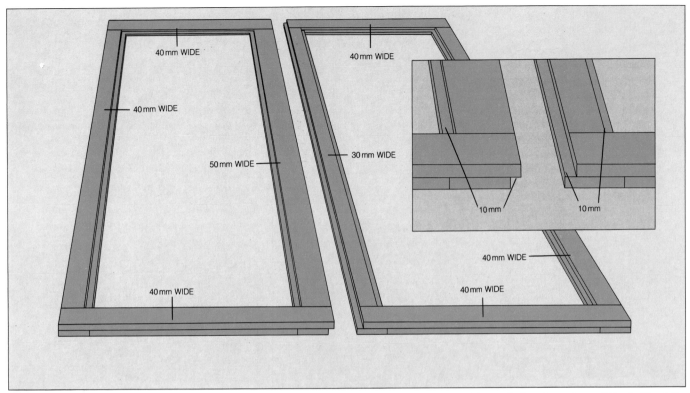

Labels on image: 40 mm WIDE, 40 mm WIDE, 40 mm WIDE, 50 mm WIDE, 40 mm WIDE, 30 mm WIDE, 40 mm WIDE, 40 mm WIDE, 10 mm, 10 mm

5 Laying out the back of the inner frames. Deduct 80 mm from the inside frame length measurement. Cut two pieces of 40 mm wide plywood, one of 50 mm wide and one of 30 mm wide, to this length. Cut two pieces of 40 mm wide plywood 10 mm shorter than the width of one front inner frame, and two pieces 10 mm longer than this width. Lay these pieces on top of the frame front so that they overlap the joints of the pieces beneath *(above)*. The different widths create a 10 mm glazing channel round the inside of the assembled frame and a meeting rebate of 10 mm along the unhinged sides *(inset)*. For a single window, cut two lengths of 40 mm wide plywood minus 80 mm each and two full widths of 40 mm.

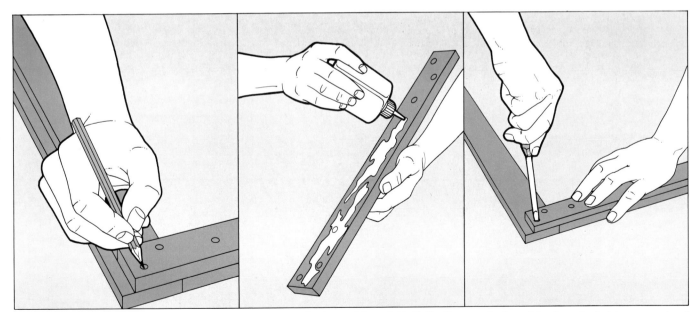

6 Joining the frames. Mark the position of the screws—two in each corner and one every 200 mm or so round the frames. The screws should be set diagonally at the corners, as far apart as possible but not less than 10 mm from the edge of the frame *(above, left)*. Drill pilot holes through the back frames only for No. 8 wood screws. Bevel the holes with a countersink bit so that the screwheads can be filled with wood filler and painted. Spread glue along the inside of each piece of the frame back *(above, centre)* and reassemble the frames. Screw the frames together, using pressure to keep the joints as tight as possible *(above, right)*. The screws will keep the wood in place while the glue hardens.

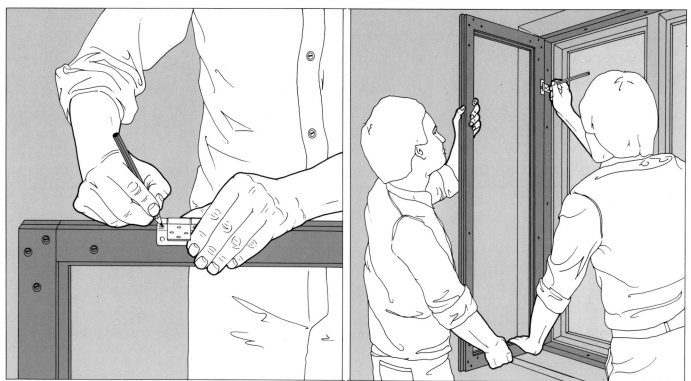

7 **Attaching the hinges.** Mark the position of the hinges through their screw holes on to the assembled inner frames. The hinges should be no more than 150 mm from the top and bottom of the frames. If the window is longer than one metre you will need three hinges. Use a bradawl to make holes for starting the screws. Screw the hinges into position.

8 **Hanging the frames.** Hold one unglazed inner frame in position on the subframe, making sure that the top and bottom are within the top and bottom rails of the subframe. While a helper supports the frame, mark the position of the hinges through the screw holes on to the subframe. Temporarily fix the inner frame with one screw at each hinge and check that the frame closes easily. Attach the second frame in the same way.

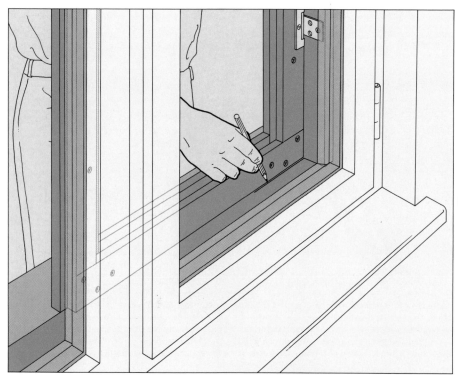

9 **Making a window stop.** Close both inner frames. Reach inside an unglazed frame and draw a line along the bottom and top of the subframe where the inner frame meets it. Fix 9 by 9 mm strips of plywood along the pencil line with panel pins. Paint all bare wooden surfaces with a coat of primer before applying the finishing paint.

10 **Glazing the inner frames.** Remove the frames from the subframe. Cut glass panes *(page 99)* to fit inside each inner frame. Line the glazing channels with a 5 mm layer of putty, smoothing the putty with a putty knife. Then press the edge of the glass into the putty.

11 **Setting the glazing pins.** Tap the glazing pins into the window frame by sliding the edge of an old chisel along the face of the glass. Space the pins at intervals of about 100 mm along all four sides of the secondary frame.

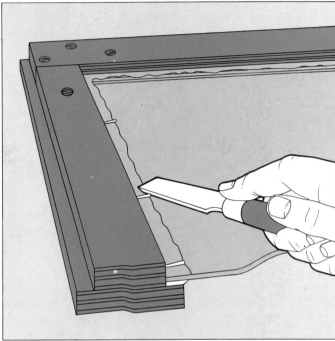

12 **Sealing the pane.** Lay enough glazing compound on the pane to fill the glazing channel. With a putty knife, bevel the compound neatly between the face of the frame and the windowpane, collecting the excess putty in your hand. Mitre the corners neatly. Clean any putty smears on the glass with methylated spirit. When the compound has hardened—after five to seven days— paint it to match the frame, extending the coat of paint just over the edge of the putty and on to the glass for a waterproof seal.

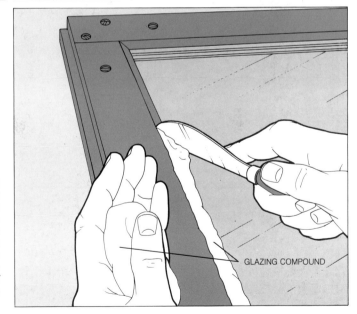

GLAZING COMPOUND

Making an Aluminium Secondary Frame

1 **Cutting the frame.** Remove the rubber gasket that comes inside the glazing channel of the frame. Measure the length and width of the window. With a pencil, mark the cutting points on the frame, making sure that each piece is slightly shorter than the glass it will cover. Check the manufacturer's instructions; the exact measurements will depend on the size of the corner pieces. Using a hacksaw with a fine-tooth blade and a mitre box, cut the pieces at right angles. File any burrs that are left by the saw.

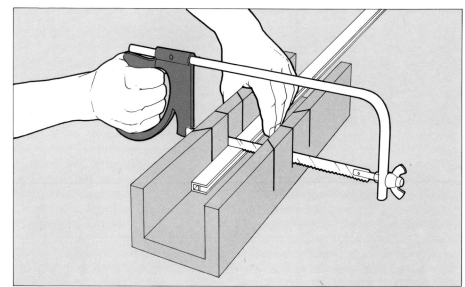

2 **Fitting the gasket.** Cut the rubber gasket with a utility knife to match the frame pieces; fit a piece of gasket to one side of the glass *(right, above)*. Centre the gasket so that the same amount of glass protrudes at the end. Take a corresponding length of frame and press it over the gasket. Place a block of wood on the middle of the frame, then tap the wood sharply with a hammer. Moving the wood first to one side, and then to the other, continue to tap it until the frame is firmly seated over the gasket and glass *(right, below)*. Fit the gasket and frame on to the opposite side of the glass and secure in the same way.

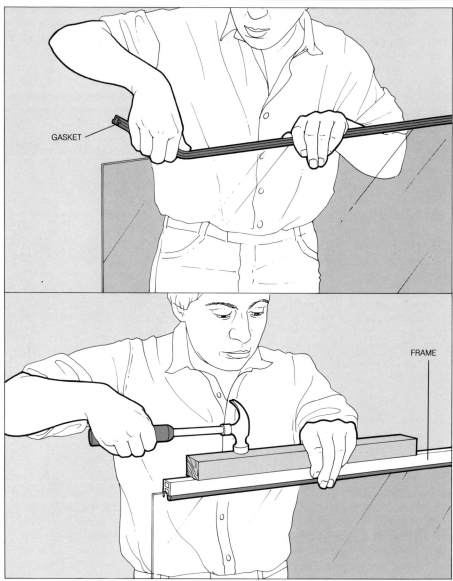

GASKET

FRAME

3 **Fitting the corner pieces.** Fit the gasket to one of the unframed sides of glass and insert a corner piece into each end of one of the remaining frame sections. Position the frame over the gasket and push the corner pieces into the ends of the two frame sections you have already fitted *(right)*. Using a hammer and wood block *(Step 2)* tap the new section into place. Secure the corner pieces with the screws supplied by the manufacturer. Fit the final section in the same way.

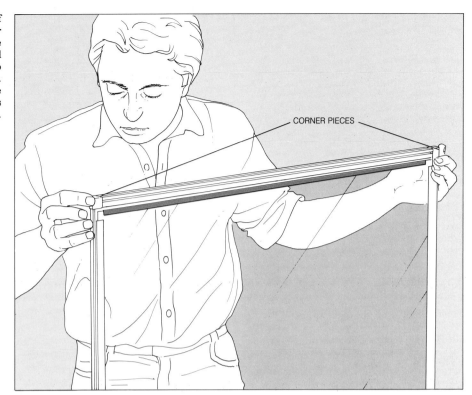

CORNER PIECES

The Delicate Art of Cutting Glass

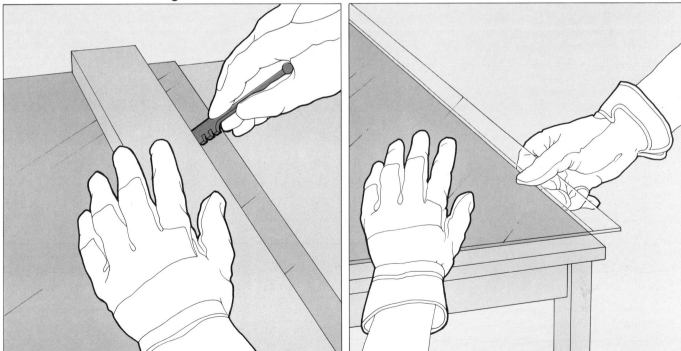

1 **Scoring glass.** Wearing gloves, lay the pane on a flat surface, and oil the cutting wheel of the glass cutter with light oil. Hold the cutter with the butt between your thumb and forefinger *(above)* and score the glass against a straightedge—a piece of wood, for example. If you begin to cut approximately 3 mm from the edge, the glass should break cleanly without chipping.

2 **Separating the glass.** Position the pane so that the score line lies along the edge of your work surface. Hold the glass against the surface with one hand and gently push on the waste piece with the other to snap the glass along the score.

Installing Insulating Glass

Replacing a single pane of glass with a sealed insulating unit—a simple form of double glazing—is not much more difficult than putting in single glazing. You will need a helper though, because of the extra weight of the glass.

First check that the rebate of your existing frame is at least 12 mm deep in order to accept the unit, and that the frame is in good condition and strong enough to take the extra weight. If the rebate is not deep enough, use a stepped unit—one pane fits inside the rebate and the other overlaps it. When ordering the glass, find out from your supplier which glazing compound is recommended for the unit. In general, you will need to use a non-hardening compound which will allow movement in the surrounding frame without cracking the glass. For installing a sealed insulating unit in a frame without beading, the technique is similar to that shown on page 97; if the window is glazed with beading, use the technique shown here.

1 Clearing the frame. Tape a dustsheet to the inside of the frame and tap the pane gently with a hammer from inside the house to fracture the glass. Wearing gloves and protective headwear, move the shards of glass back and forth to free them. Prise off the beading round the frame with a hammer and cold chisel and hammer and pull out any nails or glazing pins in the wood.

2 Removing glazing compound. Use a hammer and chisel to remove the old putty—which may be quite hard. Brush away any debris. Check the condition of the cleared frame: if the wood is damp, it should be allowed to dry out before glazing. Clean wood or metal rebates and prime them if necessary. Clear the beads of any chips of old putty, sand them smooth and prime them.

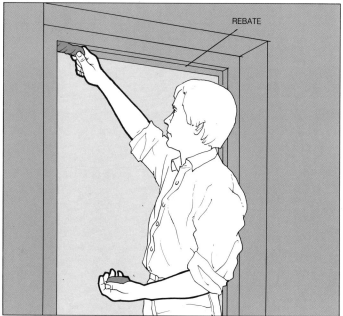

REBATE

3 Lining the frame. Line the rebate with bedding putty to a minimum depth of 5 mm. Work from the inside so that the bedding putty will be on the outside of the new glass, providing a better weatherproofing seal. For glazing with beads it is particularly important to make sure that there are no gaps in the bedding putty, so apply the putty as evenly as possible.

4 **Fitting the glass.** Clean the perimeter of the sealed unit with a dry cloth. With a helper, check the fit of the new glass in the frame. If it does not fit squarely, use plastic setting blocks to support and centre the unit *(inset)*. Position the blocks not less than 30 mm from each corner. Position the glass in the frame and press it very firmly into the bedding putty.

5 **Applying lining putty.** Apply a non-hardening glazing compound round the edge of the unit, using a putty knife. Make sure that you completely fill the clearance between the unit and the frame.

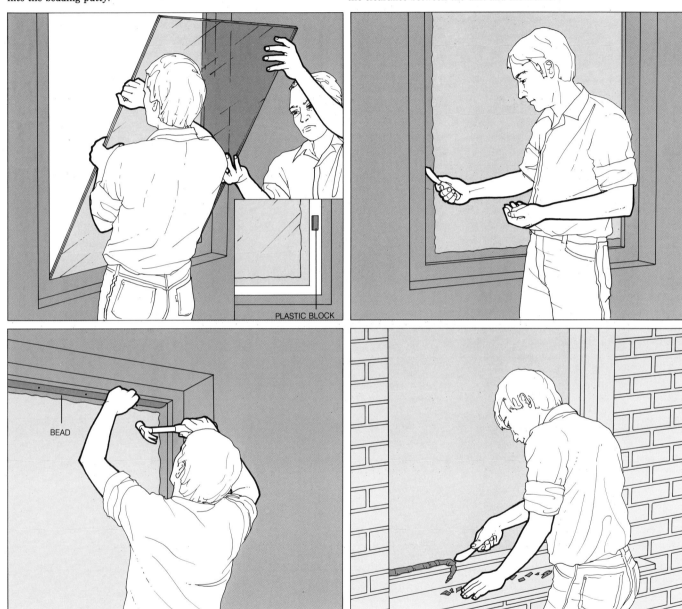

PLASTIC BLOCK

BEAD

6 **Replacing the beading.** Check the fit of the beads over the new pane—they may be a little tight. Plane or sand them to fit. Apply bedding compound to the glazing face of the beads and nail them firmly into position. Countersink the nails so that the holes can be filled and painted over. Fill cracks between the beading and the frame with ordinary hardening putty; wipe off any excess putty with a clean cloth.

7 **Cleaning the outside.** Remove any excess putty which may have been squeezed to the outside. Fill the cracks between the outside bead and the frame with ordinary hardening putty and trim off any excess with a putty knife to the sight lines. Smooth the putty with a wet knife to form an even surface. When the compound has hardened, paint it to match the frame, extending the coat of paint just on to the pane to provide a weathertight seal.

Installing Plastic Secondary Windows

If you do not wish to go to the expense of installing double glazing (page 100) or do not feel able to tackle a wooden or aluminium secondary frame (pages 93–99), you can still gain effective insulation by using one of the many secondary glazing systems which are sold in kit form and are made out of plastic. Most of these kits use PVC or acrylic sheets, a much cheaper, although less attractive, alternative to glass. A typical system consisting of a plastic frame and rigid clear plastic sheet is shown on the right. An effective secondary pane can also be made at home from plastic sheet which is cut to size and then screwed to the window moulding (below).

Whichever method you choose, make sure that there is a gap of at least 12 mm, and preferably 20 mm, between the two panes, and that both the existing window and the new one are effectively sealed against draughts. Condensation can form on the inside face of the outer pane. Since the water will damage both paint and wood, the inner pane may have to be taken out periodically to remove condensation.

Assembling and Installing a Ready-Made Window

1 Cutting the pane. For a tight, draught-free seal, the framed secondary window should be wide enough for its edges to overlap flat areas on the existing window moulding. Measure the width between flat areas. Measure the height the same way unless there is a sill. In that case, measure to the top of the sill. From these measurements subtract twice the width of the mounting frame, and use the results as dimensions for the pane.

Use a wax pencil to mark these dimensions on the plastic sheet for cutting. Place the sheet on a non-abrasive surface and, with a straight length of board as a guide, use a sharp knife to score each cutting line several times from edge to edge. Snap the sheet along the scored lines.

2 Making the frame. Cut four pieces of frame material to fit around the pane, using a mitre gauge to ensure the corners are neat. If the window has a sill, cut the bottom piece from a length of sill framing, usually supplied in the kit. Snap the frame material on to the edges of the pane.

Strip the protective tape from the frame's adhesive backing. Centre the bottom of the new window on the sill or bottom moulding of the existing window and press firmly. Working upwards, position the frame so that it sticks to the window trim. The pane can be removed by simply snapping open the frame.

Custom-Building a Window

Cutting the pane. Cut rigid clear plastic to the dimensions of the window trim as measured in Step 1 above; do not allow for a frame. If the existing window has no sill, drill pilot holes for 25 mm wood screws around the entire perimeter of the pane, 10 mm from the edge and 200 mm apart. If the window has a sill, drill holes only along the top and sides of the pane.

If there is no window sill, stick adhesive-backed weatherstripping around the entire back of the pane, alongside the edges. If the window has a sill, attach weatherstripping along the top and sides; for the base, stick it to the bottom edge so the cushion fits between the pane and sill (inset). Hold the pane against the window moulding and screw it to the moulding with 25 mm wood screws. When the window is removed for the summer, fill the screw holes with furniture plugs, available from hardware stores. The plugs can be painted to match the window trim.

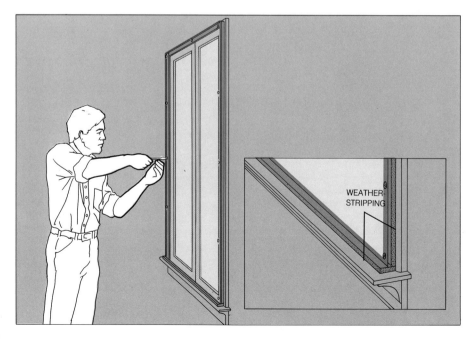

WEATHER-STRIPPING

Blinds and Shutters to Keep in the Heat

Double glazing your windows is not the only way to insulate them. Thick, lined curtains can be very effective insulators, particularly if there is a pelmet on top to prevent a cold down draught behind them, and if the bottom edge touches the floor or window sill. A special thermal lining material improves the insulating value and can also be used for other window treatments, such as the Roman blind shown here.

Even more effective are insulating shutters *(page 106)*, which are easily made from a lightweight insulating material such as rigid polystyrene slab, either fixed in a frame or sandwiched between two layers of plywood. The shutters can be folded back on hinges during the day.

Anatomy of a Roman blind. An accordion-pleated Roman blind is raised and lowered by vertical cords threaded through rings tied to the fabric and through eye screws set into a mounting board. Lowered, the blind seals the window tightly. Flexible magnetic strips sewn into the fabric edges are attached either to a metal window frame or, in the case of wooden frame windows, to matching magnetic or metal strips mounted on the moulding. A weighted metal bar holds the bottom of the blind against the sill.

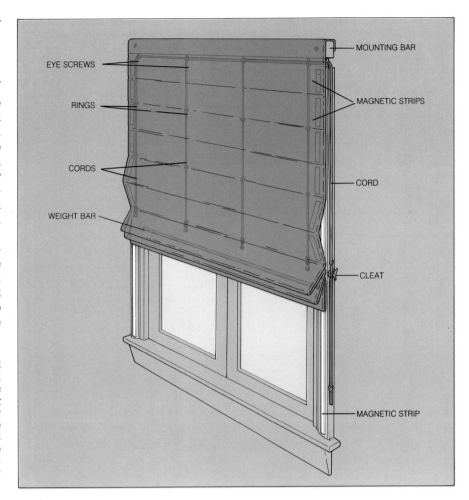

MOUNTING BAR

EYE SCREWS

RINGS

MAGNETIC STRIPS

CORDS

CORD

WEIGHT BAR

CLEAT

MAGNETIC STRIP

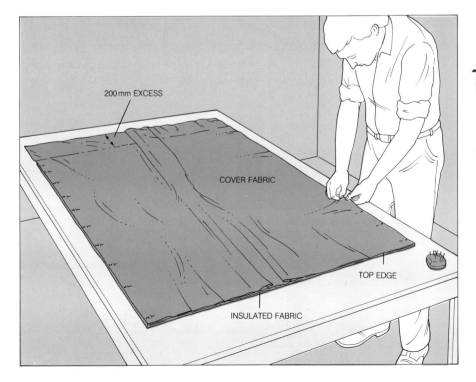

200 mm EXCESS

COVER FABRIC

TOP EDGE

INSULATED FABRIC

A Roman Blind with a Magnetic Seal

1 **Preparing the fabric.** Cut a piece of insulating fabric 100 mm longer and 50 mm wider than the dimensions of the window. (For wide windows, you may need to stitch two lengths of insulating fabric side to side.) Cut a length of decorative cover fabric—preferably sheeting or tightly woven furnishing fabric—75 mm wider and 200 mm longer than the insulating fabric.

Lay the insulating fabric with its outside face up on a table, and lay the cover fabric, face down, on top of it. Align the top and side edges of the two fabrics; pin the sides together, allowing the cover fabric's 200 mm of excess length to overhang the bottom of the insulation. Using a sewing machine, stitch a seam 10 mm in from each side of the insulating fabric; then, on each side, stitch a second, zigzag seam as close to the edges as possible, penetrating all layers of insulating fabric. The excess width of the cover fabric will lie loosely on top of the insulation.

2 **Attaching magnetic strips.** Turn the materials over so that the insulated fabric lies on top, its inside face exposed. Use tailor's chalk to mark fold lines on the sides of the blind, spacing the marks at 100 mm intervals. Cut adhesive-backed magnetic strips into 85 mm lengths, and round off the sharp corners with scissors. Place the magnets outside the straight seam on each side of the blind, centring them between the 100 mm chalk marks *(below)*. Do not put magnets at the top or bottom 100 mm of the seam lines. Fold back 100 mm of the overhang at the blind bottom, then fold another 100 mm and set two more magnets on the front side of the folded cover fabric. Turn the whole blind right side out *(top inset, below)*, so that all the magnetic strips are concealed *(bottom inset, below)* except the two on the bottom overhang, which will have unfolded. These strips will eventually be hidden by the hem. Smooth out the blind, ironing it with a cool iron if necessary.

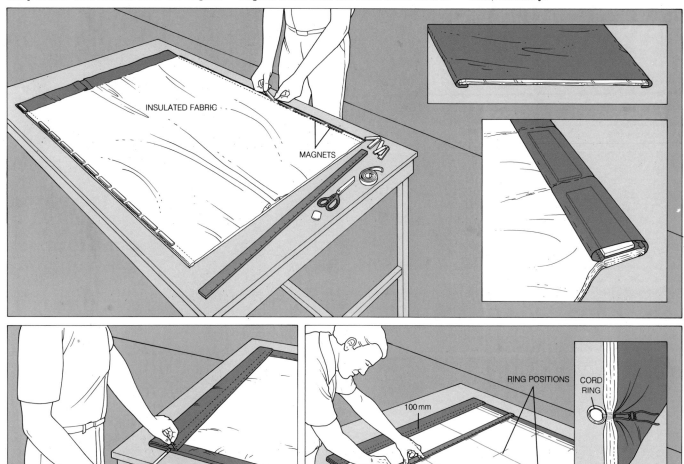

INSULATED FABRIC

MAGNETS

RING POSITIONS

CORD RING

100 mm

200 mm

200 mm

200 mm

35 mm

100 mm

3 **Weighting the hem.** With the blind right side out and face down, make a hem by again folding the overhang up 100 mm, then another 100 mm. Machine-stitch the hem along its top edge, then 25 mm below this stitching to form a channel. Cut a steel rod or a wooden batten 50 mm shorter than the width of the blind. Coat the rod with aluminium paint or varnish, and tape its ends to protect the fabric. Slide it into the channel, leaving 25 mm at each end for the bottom magnets; then hand-stitch the sides of the hem.

4 **Attaching the rings.** With tailor's chalk, mark vertical lines on the back of the blind, starting 35 mm from each edge, spacing the lines at equal intervals of 200 to 300 mm. Mark horizontal lines on the blind every 200 mm, starting 100 mm from the top. Where vertical and horizontal lines meet, sew 10 mm cord rings through all layers of fabric *(inset)* with heavy thread. Tie a reef knot and cut off the excess thread.

5 **Attaching the mounting board.** Cut a 50 by 25 mm piece of timber the width of the blind. Align it with the top of the fabric, and mark its bottom edge to correspond with each vertical row of rings. Insert 10 mm eye screws into the board at each mark, and a final one at the far left end of the board. Drill 5 mm screw holes through the board 25 mm in from each end. Then wrap the top 100 mm of the blind over the top of the board, and fasten the fabric to the wood with staples or tacks placed 50 to 75 mm apart.

6 **Stringing the cords.** For each vertical row of cord rings, cut a length of nylon blind cord about twice the length of the blind. Tie each cord to the bottom ring, securing the knot with a few drops of woodworking glue. String each cord up through its rings, threading it from right to left through the eye screws above. All of the cords will pass through the eye screw at the far left edge of the blind. Tie the cords together just beyond the last eye screw, and knot them once again about a metre down from the first knot. Trim the loose ends.

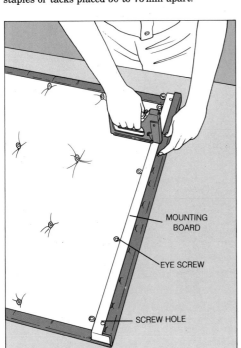

MOUNTING
BOARD

EYE SCREW

SCREW HOLE

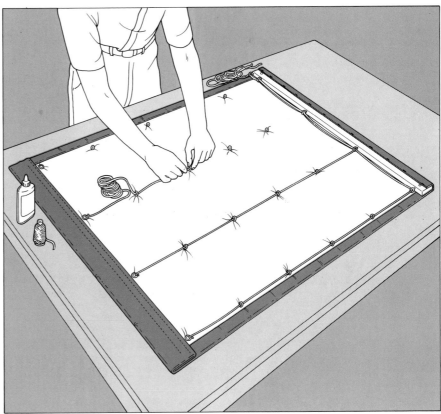

7 **Mounting the blind.** While a helper holds it at the window, check the blind for squareness and fit; adjust as needed. Uncover the screw holes on the mounting board; using 38 mm screws, attach the board to the wall above the window, leaving a clearance space for the eye screws, or to the top of the window frame.

Test the blind by pulling the lift cord firmly downwards. The blind should rise evenly in 100 mm folds that bunch loosely below the mounting board. If raising the blind is difficult, replace the last eye screw with a pulley; or attach a pulley to the wall 75 mm beyond the mounting board, then run the lift cord through the pulley. Attach a metal cleat to the wall or window casing to hold the lift cord when the blind is raised.

For a metal frame window, simply lower the blind and press its sides against the frame; the magnets will hold the blind. For wooden frame windows, clean the frames with white spirit, then mount continuous strips of magnetic tape or thin steel strips directly behind the blind edges. Press the magnets against the strips on the frame to seal the window. To break the seal, pull the blind out from the bottom.

Inside Shutters for Night-Time Warmth

Two insulated shutters. Both of these removable interior shutters cover a window with rigid foam insulation. The edges of the pop-in shutter *(below, left)* are protected by aluminium foil tape, with adhesive-backed weatherstripping at the top and bottom edges. Magnetic tape on the window side of the shutter holds it to metal shelf standards or to strips that are screwed on to the sides of the window frame. Duct-tape handles on the sides of the panel are used to break the magnetic seal when removing the shutter from the window during the day.

The more decorative bifold shutter *(below, right)* is made of two foam boards covered with wooden door panelling and hinged together. The vertical edges are covered with weatherstripping; the top and bottom edges fit against weatherstripped stops. At night, when the shutter is closed and latched, the weatherstripping seals the windows tightly. During the day, the shutter can be folded to one side.

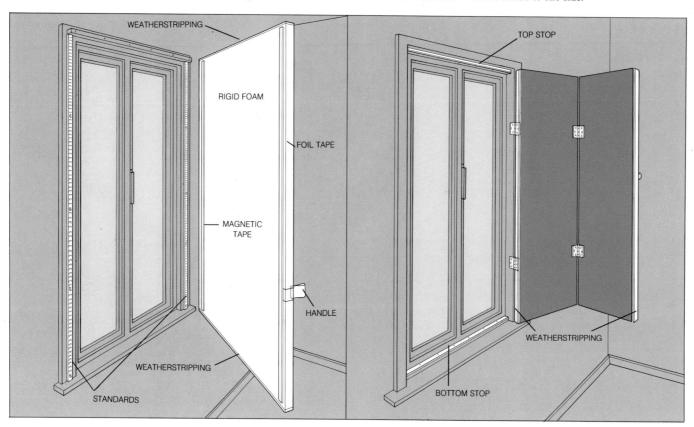

WEATHERSTRIPPING

RIGID FOAM

FOIL TAPE

MAGNETIC TAPE

HANDLE

WEATHERSTRIPPING

STANDARDS

TOP STOP

WEATHERSTRIPPING

BOTTOM STOP

Building a Bifold Shutter

1 Assembling the frames. After measuring the window, build two four-sided frames for the shutter panels, using 50 by 25 mm timber. Allow a 5 mm clearance between the outer edges of the shutter and the window frame and a fractional gap between the panels. After nailing the framing pieces together, place the frames in the window; adjust the fit if necessary.

Lay the frames on the back of a sheet of 3 mm plywood veneer, and mark the outlines, tracing each frame twice. Cut out, using a circular saw fitted with a plywood-cutting blade. Glue a cut section of veneer on to one side of each frame with woodworking adhesive. Secure the veneer to the frame with 16 mm panel pins placed at each corner and every 150 mm along the edges.

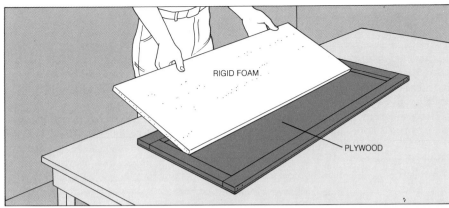

RIGID FOAM

PLYWOOD

2 **Insulating the shutter.** Cut two pieces of 20 mm rigid foam insulation to the inside measurements of the frames, allowing a slight clearance on all four sides. Lay the insulation in the frames *(left)*, and enclose the insulation with veneer. Set all the panel pins in the veneer with a nail set, fill the holes with matching wood filler, and sand the edges with fine-grade sandpaper.

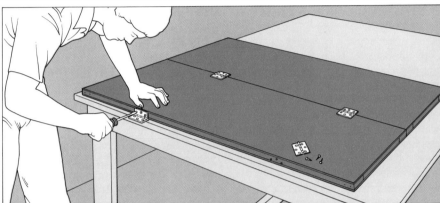

3 **Mounting the hinges.** Align the panels, outside faces up, a couple of millimetres apart. Connect them with two butt hinges equally spaced about 150 mm from top and bottom. Set two more hinges along the side edge of one shutter, aligning them with the hinges in the centre and running the knuckles along the lower edge of the panel, as shown. Screw the hinges to the panel.

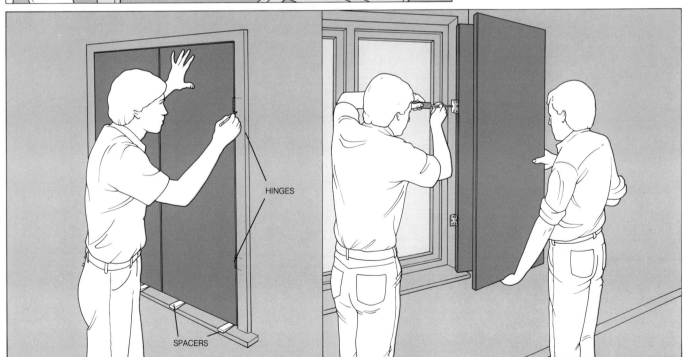

HINGES

SPACERS

4 **Hanging the shutter.** Set the closed shutter into the window frame, using wooden spacers to position it with a 5 mm clearance on all sides. Mark the hinge placements on the window casing *(above, left)*. Remove the shutter and transfer the marks to the window jamb. Next, while a helper holds the opened shutter in place, mark the position of the screw holes on the jamb. Remove the shutter and drill starter holes for the screws. Replace the shutter and screw the hinges to the jamb *(above, right)*. If necessary, cut a pair of 25 by 25 mm wood strips the width of the window, and screw them to the top and bottom of the frame to act as stops. Attach weatherstripping to the stops and to the vertical outer edges of the panels. Screw a knob to the shutter on the unhinged side, and add vertical sliding bolt latches, if necessary, to hold the shutter closed.

Thwarting the Sun with Awnings and Shields

Few settings are as inviting as a room dappled with sunshine. Yet too much sun can quickly turn a house into a hothouse, causing rugs and furniture to fade and creating unpleasant glare.

How can you block unwanted sunshine? Brightly coloured canvas awnings, once a symbol of gracious summer living, were long the favoured way. Then air conditioning permitted less cumbersome interior solutions—window hangings such as curtains and blinds. With the rising cost of electricity, however, awnings have made a comeback. Awnings reflect heat before it has a chance to enter a room, and cool more effectively than blinds or curtains, which may actually absorb heat and trap it indoors. Used alone, awnings lower interior temperatures by up to 8°C; used in combination with air conditioning, they markedly reduce power consumption.

When you are choosing awnings, carefully consider the material they are made of. Canvas is least expensive, but it fades, tends to shrink and does not resist fire. More practical—though more costly—are awnings that are made of coated cottons or synthetics. Vinyl-coated, 100 per cent spun polyester lasts longer than plain canvas and also has greater resistance to both fire and mould.

The colour of an awning is important to its efficiency. White fabric awnings, tested over plate-glass windows on the side of a house facing the sun, have proved nearly 10 per cent more effective than dark green ones. Style, too, has practical as well as aesthetic value. Awnings with sides—called wings—protect windows from peripheral sunlight, but they also trap heat and slow the release of warm air from inside the house. Retractable awnings, which can be raised or lowered according to the sun's position, offer obvious advantages over the fixed variety, which permanently block both light and view.

On the following pages are installation procedures for typical ready-made canopy or cassette-type awnings. They are available in standard sizes—the measurements shown below indicate the minimum size you should buy—and they are purchased in kits which include all the hardware necessary for installation. When mounting awnings on brick walls, be sure to use metal wall anchors into which wood screws can be threaded. Since details vary considerably depending on the size, style and brand of awning, read the manufacturer's instructions carefully.

If the cost or appearance of awnings makes them undesirable, an alternative is a tinted plastic film applied with water to the inner side of window glass. Depending on the brand, this shield may be held in place either by self-adhesion or by electrostatic pressure (the same force that causes a briskly rubbed balloon to adhere to a wall). These shields deflect exterior heat so well that, in some cases, air-conditioning needs are cut by half. The tinted film reduces visibility only slightly, and it virtually eliminates glare and the ultra-violet rays that cause furnishings to fade. This method has only two major disadvantages: it lowers the daytime light level in a room, and when the windows are opened to admit breezes, sunlight pours in unchecked. But the ease of installation and low price make tinted plastic film a practical solution for many home owners.

Measuring for Awnings

Sash windows. To determine the length of the awning drop, measure from the top of the casing to a point half way down the window. For awnings with wings, measure the width from midpoint to midpoint of the side casings; for wingless awnings, measure the width of the window sash, then add 200 mm. Measure in the same way for inward-opening casement windows.

Casement windows. For outward-opening casement windows, measure the projection—the distance from the wall to the outermost point on the window when it is fully opened—then measure the drop and width as you would for sash windows. Casement awnings are usually mounted higher than sash types. Retailers have charts to help you to make the appropriate adjustment.

Installing a Canopy Awning

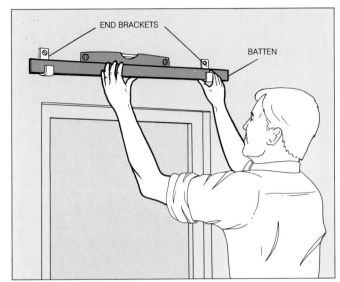

END BRACKETS

BATTEN

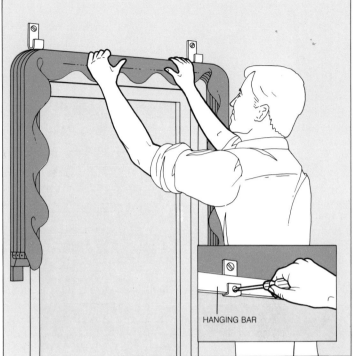

HANGING BAR

1 Positioning the brackets. Measure the width of the awning and transfer the measurement to the wall above the window. Guided by the manufacturer's instructions, mark fixing points for the two end brackets about 120 mm from either end of the awning. Fix the first end bracket with the screws and plugs provided and check with a spirit level that it is vertical.

Place one end of a piece of battening wood the same width as the awning into the fixed bracket. Hold a second bracket around the other end of the batten and, using a spirit level, adjust the batten until it is level *(above)*. Mark the position for the second bracket and fix it to the wall. Use the batten for marking the positions for any intermediate brackets along the same line.

2 Hanging the awning. Lift the awning above the window *(above)* and drop the hanging bar at the back of the frame on to the brackets. Centre the awning over the window by sliding it sideways. Then, working beneath the opened awning, drill pilot holes through each bracket and the hanging bar. Insert self-tapping screws into the holes to secure the bar *(inset)*. If the awning legs to do not have detachable castings *(Step 3)*, mark and drill the holes for the castings before fitting the self-tapping screw into the hanging bar.

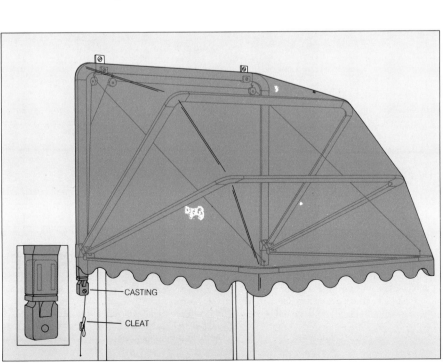

CASTING

CLEAT

3 Completing the installation. Slip a metal casting into the bottom of each leg of the awning and mark the positions for the fixing screws through the holes. Remove the castings; drill and plug the wall, replace the castings and fix them securely to the wall. Fix a cord cleat to the wall below one of the legs and, following the manufacturer's instructions, thread the cord through the pulleys. Open and shut the awning several times to check that it is working correctly.

Installing Cassette Awnings

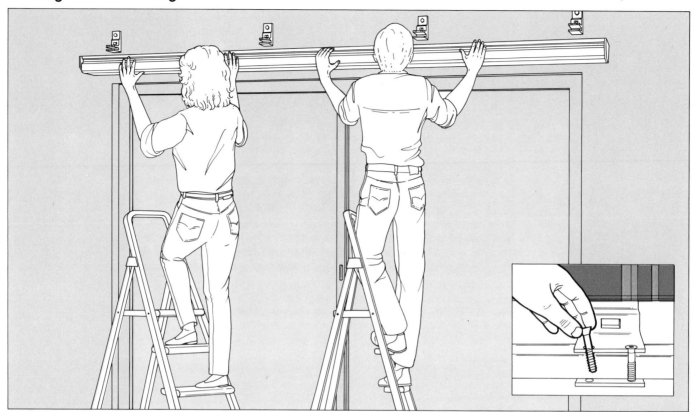

1 **Hanging the awning.** Mark positions for the brackets above the window *(Step 1, page 109)*. Using a masonry drill, fix the brackets to the wall with the coach screws provided by the manufacturer. With a helper, lift the awning *(above)* until it is level with the brackets, then slot the carrier bar at the back of the awning between the two teeth of each bracket. Push the carrier bar until it touches the back of the brackets. Pull the awning open to a maximum of 300 mm to allow access; drop two retaining screws into the holes pre-cut in each bracket *(inset)* and tighten the screws with an allen key. The awning must not be fully opened until the screws have been secured in the brackets.

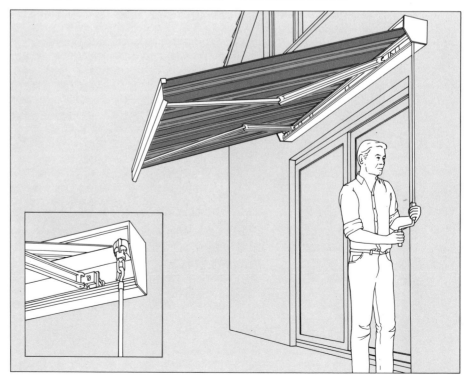

2 **Operating the awning.** Hook the crooked end of the cranking handle into the eye attached to the gear case *(inset)* and turn the handle to extend the awning fully. Close and open the awning several times to check that it is correctly balanced and working properly.

Plastic Sunglasses for Windows

1 Preparing the window. Wash the inside of the window thoroughly. Scrape off any adhering grit with a blade and wash the glass again. Cut the tinted plastic film slightly larger than the glass. Mist the glass with water, peel the protective liner from the film, and mist the side of the film that will rest against the window. Apply the film to the glass, mist and then lightly squeegee the surface.

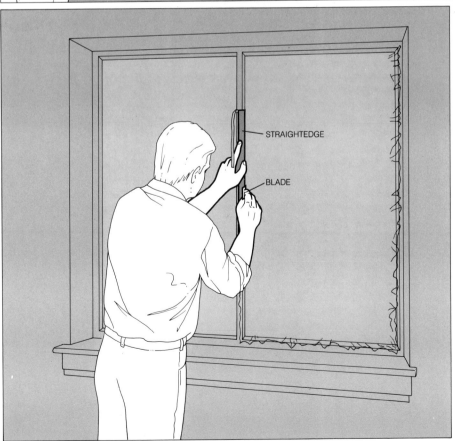

2 Trimming the film. Butt a straightedge against the window frame, with the edge on the glass. Using a sharp blade, trim the film along the straightedge, thus creating a narrow border of glass round the film. Mist the film again, and squeegee from the top down to remove as much water as possible from beneath the film. Finish by drying the edges of the glass with a lint-free cloth. The window will be hazy until all moisture trapped behind the film evaporates by way of the narrow border round the film—a process that may take more than a week.

Dealing with the Timber-Eaters

Wet rot. A crowbar lifts a timber board that has been destroyed by an advanced attack of wet rot. The damp penetrated the adjacent brick wall and eventually soaked the timber floor. Poor ventilation of the sub-floor area created an ideal environment for the wet rot fungus to flourish. Once the source of damp has been identified—in this case, a faulty damp-proof course—and corrected, air bricks or a grille should be set into the wall below the floor level and damaged timber replaced. When all the boards are dry, the whole area should be treated with rot-destroying fluid.

A house faces assault not only from the elements, but also from a host of natural invaders such as birds, rodents and insects. Some of these pests are merely annoying, but others can be devastatingly destructive—and none more so than the insects and fungi which feed on wood. Indeed, it has been calculated that the timber-eaters are second only to fire as a threat to the structure of our houses.

The most voracious of these predators are the termites, or so-called white ants, which can be found in hotter climates in places as far apart as Adelaide and Avignon. They live in large subterranean colonies and reach a food source either by tunnelling through the earth or by building mud-covered runways. Constructed over the surface of brick, concrete or steel, and rising perhaps many metres above the ground, these enclosed runways enable the termites to avoid exposure to dry air. If you discover such runways during an inspection of your house, call in a professional termite eradicator.

Less dangerous but more widespread are the various types of wood-boring beetle *(pages 114–115)*. In fact, most of the damage is done by the beetles' larvae, which hatch from eggs laid on the surface of timber. The larvae, known appropriately as woodworm, bore down into the timber, tunnelling away for several years until eventually they become adults and chew their way out.

Serious problems are also posed by two types of wood-decaying fungi—wet rot and dry rot *(pages 118–121)*. Wet rot is the more prevalent and develops in places where timber is in contact with persistently wet surroundings—in a leaking attic or a damp basement, for example. Dry rot also requires an external moisture supply in its early stages. Once established, however, it can spread from wet to dry timber, pass over brickwork, and travel through mortar joints and behind plaster. Moreover, in damp, ill-ventilated conditions, the growth rate of dry rot is so rapid that it can infect an entire house in as little as three months.

Since many wood-boring insects also flourish in damp conditions, it is essential to make sure that your house remains free from moisture. Carry out regular maintenance inspections *(pages 22-23)*; repair all plumbing leaks, replace broken or missing roof tiles and keep gutters clear so that they do not overflow.

In the event of rot or woodworm being discovered, the affected areas will need to be thoroughly sterilized. Bear in mind, however, that this can be a long and laborious process, and you may well prefer to leave it to the professionals. Many firms offer free inspections and estimates, and in most cases the treatment is guaranteed for 30 years. Fees for such work vary widely, so it is worth obtaining at least two estimates. Arrange that these are broken down to show not only the anticipated labour costs, but the rate per hour. You will then be able to check that the amount shown on the invoice tallies with the amount of work actually put in.

Waging War on the Wood-Borers

Most of the decay in building timbers is caused by woodworm—the larvae of various types of wood-boring insect. Three of these insects are described opposite. Other borers include the wood-boring weevil, the New Zealand weevil and the death-watch beetle—known by its characteristic tapping noise, which is made by knocking its head against wood to attract a mate.

All these pests have a similar life cycle (*below*) and all are encouraged by damp, infesting such places as skirting boards, roofing and flooring timbers, and understairs cupboards. However, some species have a preference for wood which is already weakened by fungal decay. The death-watch beetle, for example, is one which will attack only hardwoods, especially oak, which have been affected by a fungus. The wood-boring weevil and the New Zealand weevil also confine themselves to wood that has been attacked by a fungus, usually wet rot. In contrast, the common furniture beetle can eat virtually any type of wood, which accounts for the fact that this beetle does more damage than all the other wood-borers put together.

It is during the summer months, when the newly formed adults leave the wood to mate, that you should look for signs of infestation—tiny flight holes and small piles of fresh-looking bore dust or "frass" on the surface of the wood.

Since a thorough inspection of the whole house is bound to entail a good deal of upheaval, you should try to combine it with spring-cleaning or redecorating. In this way you will save yourself the trouble of shifting furniture and taking up floor coverings on two separate occasions. Work your way systematically through the whole house, paying particular attention to any areas that may be damp—around baths, sinks and W.C.s, for example. If you discover woodworm and rot together, apply the treatment for rot (*pages 118–121*), using a combination fluid of both fungicide and insecticide.

In the case of woodworm attack, you must first cut away any badly weakened timber, which should be burned immediately to avoid spreading infestation. You must then kill the woodworm in the remaining timber with an insecticidal fluid, either injecting it into the flight holes or brushing or spraying it on to the surface.

By far the easiest method is spraying. You can use a pressurized garden spray with an extension lance for less accessible areas— for example, in the eaves or under the floorboards. For best results, two coats should be applied, the second after the first has been absorbed.

Woodworm fluid gives off a pungent odour, so make sure the room is well ventilated before you start spraying. Wear overalls or old clothes, a face mask, goggles and heavy-duty protective gloves. Do not wear rubber gloves—some woodworm fluids attack rubber. If you are working in the attic (*overleaf*), you should also wear a safety helmet, which will protect you from banging your head on the rafters.

Woodworm fluid is highly inflammable and there must be no naked flames or smoking in the area either during treatment or in the 48 hours following. Have a fire extinguisher handy while you are spraying. If you need lighting in an attic or basement, run it from a socket in another part of the house, with no switch in the lead. Sparks produced by a faulty switch are liable to ignite the fumes from the fluid. Alternatively, use a torch.

Life Cycle of a Wood-Borer

From egg to adult. The life cycles of the different kinds of wood-boring insect vary considerably in length, but they are all marked by the same four distinct stages, described here for a common furniture beetle (*left*). First, the adult female lays her eggs—up to 80 at a time—in the cracks, crevices and joints of rough timber, as well as in old flight holes. After three to five weeks, the eggs hatch into larvae, which immediately begin to burrow into the wood.

Nourished by the cellulose in the wood, each larva tunnels for three to four years, eating about 50 mm of wood a year. The larva then makes a cavity near the surface and changes into a chrysalis. After six to eight weeks, the adult beetle emerges from the chrysalis and chews its way out of the wood in order to mate. The male usually dies within a day of mating, but the female survives until she has laid her eggs—thus ensuring that the life cycle continues.

Tracking a Deadly Trio

The common furniture beetle. By far the most prevalent of the wood-boring insects, the common furniture beetle measures about 3 mm and is dark brown in colour. The adults emerge from the timber during the late spring and summer; on warm days you may see them flying around or crawling on walls, ceilings and windows.

The beetles live for two to three weeks after emerging, so the females have plenty of time to mate and deposit their eggs over a wide area. Their flight holes, circular and perfectly formed, are about 1.5 mm in diameter. These holes and the accompanying piles of bore dust are the tell-tale signs of attack. You should watch out for them not only in furniture, but also in floorboards (including the underside), skirting boards, joists and rafters.

The powder post beetle. This insect derives its name from the ability of the larvae to reduce timber to a fine, flour-like powder. Adults have the same dark brown colouring as the common furniture beetle, but are thinner and longer, measuring about 6 mm. Their life cycle is short, with less than a year spent in the wood. Like the furniture beetle, they make neat, circular flight holes about 1.5 mm in diameter, though their bore dust is finer. They emerge from late spring through to the end of the summer and they fly mainly at dusk.

Because of their preference for recently cut hardwoods such as oak, elm and ash, the beetles are a particular menace in timber yards and other places where fresh wood is stored. However, their targets also include panelling, flooring and furniture made of fresh hardwood.

The house longhorn beetle. Ranging from 12 to 25 mm in length, the adult beetle is greyish-black, with a small greyish mark on each wing case. It emerges during the summer months, leaving an irregular oval slit in the timber which can be up to 6 mm long.

The grubs have a particularly long life cycle, often tunnelling in the wood for 10 years before the onset of pupation. As a result, they can virtually destroy the inside of a piece of timber before any outward signs of decay are apparent. It used to be thought that the house longhorn attacked only well-seasoned softwood, but there is now evidence that it also attacks hardwoods.

Treating Woodworm

1 **Assessing the damage.** To find out how seriously the wood has been weakened by woodworm, poke it with the point of a screwdriver *(above)*. If the wood feels firm, it can be treated. If the wood feels soft, consult a professional; you may have to cut out and burn the damaged piece.

2 **Cleaning the wood.** Wearing goggles and a mask to protect your eyes and mouth, rub down the surface with a stiff brush *(above)*—dirt will inhibit the effectiveness of the woodworm fluid. Vacuum the dust. Cover water tanks and electric cables with polythene sheeting, and remove insulating material from between the joists. This should be replaced only after the fluid has dried out, which normally takes about a week.

3 **Applying the fluid.** Using a pressurized garden sprayer, with an extension lead for out-of-the-way surfaces, spray the affected area and surrounding timber. If dealing with only a small area, it may be more convenient either to brush on the fluid or inject it directly into the flight holes, using a proprietary injector with a specially designed nozzle.

Before starting work, check that the sprayer is fitted with a moderately coarse nozzle. If the nozzle is too fine, the fluid may vaporize; if it is too coarse, the wood will be drenched. The application rate for the fluid depends on the brand, but it is generally 1 litre to 4 square metres of timber. Spray all the timber, not just the obviously affected parts, paying particular attention to cracks, joints and end grain. Apply a second coat after the first has been absorbed. Leave the fluid to soak in for 24 hours, then wipe off any excess with a dry, clean cloth. Treat new timbers before putting them in place.

How to Combat Mould

Mould requires very little nutrient and will grow on almost any surface that is persistently damp—from brick, plaster and paint to linoleum, wallpaper and clothing. Germinated from minute spores that float through the air, mould first appears as small spots or patches of various colours. These spots then spread to form a furry layer on the surface. If the surface is painted, the mould may grow within the paint film itself, causing a pink or purple stain.

Although mould is unsightly rather than harmful, it is usually the sign of a serious condensation problem which should be treated. First, you should reduce the amount of water vapour that is created—for example, by drying clothes in the garden and by keeping the bathroom door shut when taking a bath. Second, you should ventilate the house so that the moist air is constantly replaced with currents of drier air from the outside.

Opening the windows may help, but a much better solution is to provide suitable vents in attics and basements, and to install extractor fans or dehumidifiers in moisture-prone areas such as kitchens and bathrooms *(pages 60–67)*. However, neither of these steps will be effective unless surface temperatures are kept at a fairly high level—which is one reason for ensuring adequate insulation *(Chapter 3)*.

Having dealt with the underlying causes, you can then go on to treat the mould outbreak itself *(below)*. Various brands of toxic wash are available. These will not only destroy the mould, but will also sterilize the area treated against further outbreaks.

Decorations will usually need stripping off before the wash is applied, although some finishes, such as oil-based distemper, will absorb treatment without damage. Undecorated surfaces, including external walls, need no preparation, but may require a final rinsing with water to get rid of discoloration caused by the wash.

Toxic washes should be applied with scrupulous care. Follow the manufacturer's instructions and always wear protective clothing. Many of them are caustic in concentrated solutions, and even solutions diluted ready for use can be dangerous if splashed on the skin.

Treating an inside wall. Strip off any wallpaper from the affected area. If the area has been coated with paint, this should also be removed unless it is one of the few types capable of absorbing a fungicide. Scrub the surface with a household detergent and brush on the toxic wash *(left)*.

The main ingredient comes as a liquid or powder concentrate and must be diluted and applied strictly according to the manufacturer's instructions. Wear protective goggles and gloves. Leave the wash to soak in for at least a week; if any signs of new growth appear, repeat the treatment. Allow the surface to dry out completely before redecorating the wall.

Eradicating Wood-Rotting Fungi

Next to woodworm, the greatest threat to building timbers comes from two types of fungal decay—wet rot and dry rot. Wet rot—caused almost entirely by the so-called cellar fungus, *Coniophora puteana*—is by far the more common of the two but, since it remains confined to wood that is actually damp, it is also the easiest to deal with.

In contrast, dry rot—caused by the dry rot fungus, *Serpula lacrymans*—is able to transfer itself from damp to dry wood, as well as to substances that give it no nourishment, such as brick, mortar and plaster.

Like all fungi, wet and dry rot reproduce themselves by means of tiny spores given off by fruiting bodies, or sporophores. A spore, having fallen on damp wood, then develops a mass of root-like strands, known as hyphae, which break down the cellulose in the timber for food. The mature fungus eventually produces a fruiting body of its own and this, in turn, releases more spores, thus continuing the life cycle.

Rot usually begins where timber is in direct contact with damp brickwork or concrete—in outside door and window frames, for example, or in joists or floorboards alongside an exterior wall *(overleaf)*—and where ventilation is inadequate. The most obvious signs of decay are warping and shrinkage of the wood; in advanced cases, fungal strands, fruiting bodies and spores may be visible on the surface of the wood. Dry rot often produces a pungent odour similar to that of mushrooms. In a timber floor, wide gaps may also appear between the skirting and floorboards.

Before applying any treatment, you must make sure that the source of damp has been eradicated and that the timbers are fully dried out. Areas beneath suspended timber floors at ground level should be well ventilated to avoid the accumulation of moisture. Where necessary, install new air grilles and bricks *(page 65)*; check that existing ones are not blocked. If these precautions are not taken, the problem will simply return.

You must also make sure that the type of rot has been correctly established. Applying wet rot treatment to dry rot will not only be a waste of time and money, but may actually cause the infestation to spread more rapidly. On the other hand, applying dry rot treatment to wet rot will certainly effect a cure, but it will also be needlessly expensive.

When attempting to identify the type of rot, there are a number of distinguishing features to watch out for *(opposite)*. Dry rot has thick, grey hyphae which mat together to form fluffy, cotton wool-like masses and eventually flat, grey sheets, known as mycelium. These sheets often show patches of lemon yellow and tinges of lilac. Droplets of water may also collect on the surface—which accounts for the dry rot fungus being named *lacrymans* (from the Latin, "weeping").

Where mycelium has accumulated sufficient food reserves or is under "stress" through having moved some distance from the germination site, fruiting bodies develop and release their quota of rust-coloured spores. These are produced in such abundance that the surrounding surfaces soon become coated with what looks like a fine, red dust. Yet each spore is only 0.01 mm long and 20,000 million are needed to cover 1 square metre.

In the case of wet rot, the hyphae resemble thin string or twine and often grow in a dark, vein-like pattern. Surface mycelium is rarely produced, though in some locations—for example, under impermeable floor coverings or behind skirting boards—a greyish sheet similar to that of *Serpula* may develop. Elsewhere, the mycelium sometimes appears as a yellowish or dark brown skin.

Although fruiting bodies are seldom found in buildings, they may be common out of doors on trees and fallen branches. They consist of small, rounded tubercles or irregular lumps which turn from creamy yellow to olive brown as the spores are formed. Unlike the spores of *Serpula*, those

of wet rot fungi are rarely seen in any accumulation. Instead, they drift invisibly in the air, searching out any timber with a sufficiently high moisture content—between 38 and 42 per cent.

Because wet rot is unable to spread beyond the immediate source of damp, it is fairly easy to establish the extent of any attack. Finding out how far dry rot has spread is much harder. It can infest timber with a moisture content of only 20 per cent—and, once established, dry rot can pass over or through any surface.

Each type of rot requires a different treatment. You can kill the wet rot fungus simply by removing the source of damp and allowing the affected surfaces to dry out. However, to ensure against the risk of a fresh outbreak should the area again become damp, it is advisable to use replacement timbers that have been pretreated with a preservative. In addition, all timber left intact should be sterilized with a fungicidal solution; like woodworm fluid, this can be applied with an ordinary pressurized garden spray *(overleaf)*. Access to underfloor areas can be gained by lifting every sixth floorboard.

Treatment for dry rot is much more difficult and should always be left to the professionals. As well as cutting out the infected timber, it is also necessary to remove surrounding plaster and mortar to ensure that every trace of the fungus is found. Following this, all surfaces contaminated with rot, including brickwork, must be cleaned down with a wire brush and treated with a fungicidal solution.

Most areas can be sterilized by spraying, but where a wall is more than 115 mm thick it must be sterilized through the process known as "irrigation". This process, which is also used for installing a chemical damp-proof course *(pages 44–47)*, is best left to a professional in the case of dry rot. All replacement timber should again be pretreated with a preservative and any refurbishments should be carried out using fungicidal plaster and paint.

The Signs of Wet Rot and Dry Rot

Wet rot. Often, there is little or no visible evidence of growth on the wood, but in very advanced cases of wet rot you may see thread-like strands, which turn from yellowish to dark brown or black *(above)*. Infected wood becomes darker and cracks across the grain *(inset)*, though damage may be invisible beneath a layer of sound wood or paint.

Dry rot. Grey strands, sometimes as thick as a pencil, spread to form fluffy masses and eventually—in advanced severe attacks of dry rot—vast, sheet-like growths known as mycelium *(above, left)*. These can develop pancake-shaped fruiting bodies, which are greyish white at the edges and rust-coloured at their spore-bearing centres *(above, right)*. Infected wood is brown and heavily cubed—that is, cracked both along and across the grain *(inset)*.

Curing Wet Rot in a Timber Floor

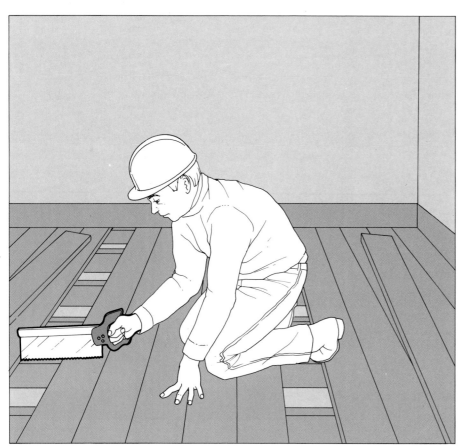

1 Removing the rotten timber. Prod the timber surrounding the affected area to test for hidden infestation, using a pointed instrument such as a penknife or screwdriver. If the wood is rotten the point will slip in easily; sound timber will resist both insertion and withdrawal.

Lift every sixth floorboard to check for infestation under the floor. If the joists themselves are rotten you will probably need to engage a professional builder. Locate the position of electric cables and then cut away all damaged timber well beyond the signs of decay. Using a floorboard cutter—available from tool suppliers—or a handsaw *(left)*, saw through boards where they run across joists. Put the rotten timber and all sweepings into a polythene bag and burn it as soon as possible.

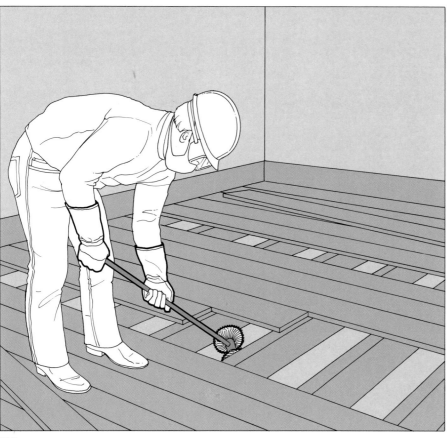

2 Cleaning the wood. Rub down all surfaces with a stiff brush above and beneath the boards *(left)*, then remove the dirt with a nozzle-type vacuum cleaner. Protect yourself from flying dust with goggles, face mask and gloves. Protect any rubber-covered cables or junction boxes with a sealant—some brands of fungicide attack rubber—and isolate electrical currents.

3 **Applying the fungicide.** Spray the entire floor, above and underneath, with a proprietary fungicide specially formulated for treating dry rot. This should be applied with a coarse nozzle attached to either a pressurized garden spray or a hydraulic pump. Follow the manufacturer's instructions for the strength of the solution and the exact amount to use. When the first application has been absorbed, spray a second time. Always wear a safety helmet, face mask, goggles and heavy-duty protective gloves (not rubber) when spraying. Have a fire extinguisher handy.

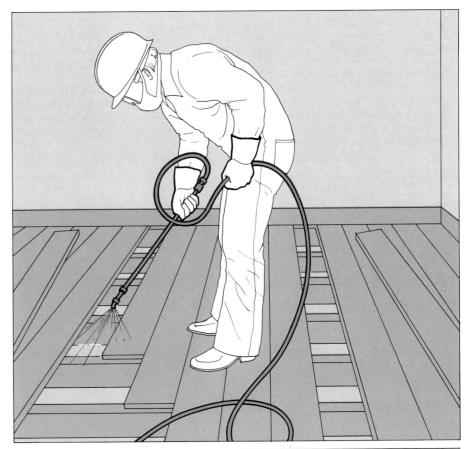

4 **Replacing timber.** Cut replacement boards to size. Brush two coats of fungicide on to the new boards and also on the boards you have removed to gain access; allow the first coat to be absorbed before applying the second. Steep the sawn ends in the fluid for at least 10 minutes before fixing in place. If you are replacing joists, paint the ends with bituminous paint suitable for wood. Allow all surfaces to dry out completely before replacing floor coverings and furnishings.

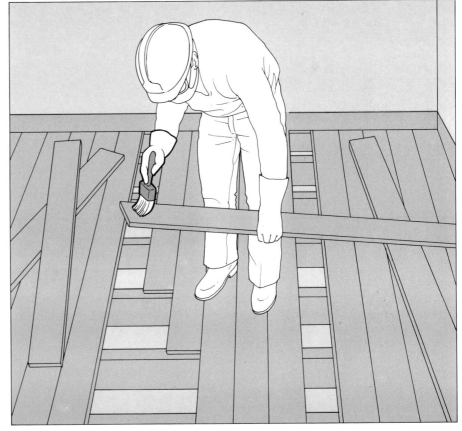

A Seasonal Checklist for a Snug House

Emergency repairs come at the wrong time, in the wrong weather, when tools and materials to do them properly seem to be missing. If you do not wait for the emergency but tackle each job at the appropriate time, you can make minor repairs before they become major ones. The following calendar indicates the seasons best suited for the maintenance that will keep your house weathertight.

Spring

Gutters
The weight of winter snow and ice can force gutters out of alignment or start leaks at low points. During a heavy spring shower, look for drips and points of overflow—or, in dry weather, run water through the gutters from a garden hose. Check also that the gutters and cages above downpipes are not clogged with leaves and debris. Reposition screws or brackets to return a gutter to the correct pitch; scrape rusted spots clean with a wire brush and coat both the rusted area and the surface immediately around it with rust-resistant primer or bitumen paint. A small crack or hole can be stopped with an epoxy repair material or patched with an aluminium sealing strip, but if a gutter is pitted with many holes or has rusted through in long seams, replace the entire section *(pages 36–37).*

Roofs
Replace damaged or dislodged tiles, and make any repairs necessary to damaged roofing felt and battens *(pages 24–27).* Slates with fine cracks can sometimes be repaired with bituminous mastic or a metal patch, but a badly damaged slate must be replaced: use a slate ripper to remove the nails that hold it in place and substitute a new slate cut to the correct size and secured with a strip of metal flashing *(pages 28–29).* On a flat roof, check for blisters and make any repairs necessary before water gets through the roof sheathing. Cut each blister open, dry the underlying felt if necessary, and seal the cut with a patch of roofing felt and cold mastic *(pages 30–31).* Finally, check the condition of all metal flashing on the roof, especially round chimneys. Remove rust spots with a wire brush and seal loose joints with bituminous mastic. Repair small cracks with metal patches, or replace the entire section if the damage is extensive *(pages 32–33).* For all work that is carried out on the roof, it is essential to follow the safety guidelines listed on page 27.

Bird Nests
Some nests are welcome, others can be a nuisance. If birds construct their nests in areas important to the ventilation or weatherproofing of your house—for example, against an attic vent or the outer cover of a venting fan—remove the nest. Recheck the spot periodically for the remainder of the season—other birds are likely to find the same good nesting place.

Lightning Protection
If you live in an area subject to summer electrical storms, make your annual inspection of your lightning-protection system, but do not try to repair the system yourself—an amateur repair can be more dangerous than the defect itself. If any terminals, ground rods, cables, conductors or clamps are loose, damaged or completely missing, consult a professional electrician or your local electricity board.

Summer

Woodworm
During the warm months of late spring and summer, the adults of the most common species of wood-boring insects emerge from the timber they have infested; sometimes they can be seen crawling or flying around. Check all floorboards, skirting boards, cupboards, joists, rafters and wooden furniture for their tell-tale flight holes and small piles of bore dust. Damp areas are especially vulnerable to infestation by certain species. The damage caused by the larvae—which tunnel inside the wood for periods of several years before emerging as beetles—is often much worse than the visible evidence may suggest. Consult a professional if the wood yields readily to the point of a penknife or screwdriver; firm wood can be treated with insecticidal fluid *(page 116).*

Insect Nests
By early summer, most bee and wasp nests are well established, but still small enough to be easily removed. Look for them at eaves or under-roof areas; use binoculars on the outside of the house to check eave or soffit vents or look from inside an attic to see if insects have worked their way into the louvres of a roof or attic vent. If you discover a nest, do not attempt to remove it while it is still inhabited—first kill the insects with a spray, then knock the nest down and thoroughly clean the area to which it was fastened.

Vent Blockages

On a hot day you should be able to perceive rising currents of air starting at soffit vents in the eaves and moving towards the higher vents on a gable roof; if you do not, clean the vents—they may be clogged with leaves—and make sure that the insides of the vents are not blocked by furniture stored in the attic.

Kitchen Fans

In summer grease builds up fast but is easily removed. Wash the filter, then take out the motor-and-fan assembly (in most models the assembly is secured by two or three screws and the motor can be disconnected by pulling a plug). Use a solution of household detergent to clear all surfaces of grease, but do not submerge the motor. Be careful not to bend fan blades, which are usually thin. Before replacing the assembly, oil the motor and clean the housing.

Moisture

At points where wood meets other materials, or where a wooden structure such as a porch meets the main house, look for water damage indicated by flaking or blistered paint. (Remember that water can flow along these seams for some distance before lodging and damaging wood or paint.) Choose an appropriate sealant material *(pages 16–17)* to caulk the points at which water penetrated the joints, and apply it on a warm, dry day. Do not try to touch up the paint that still adheres directly over the moist wood. First remove the blistered or loose paint and let the wood dry thoroughly; if moisture has raised a nap on the damp wood, sand the area smooth before repainting.

Autumn

Caulking

The freezing water of winter, which can expand inside or alongside a caulked seam, is even harder on areas where different construction materials adjoin than the warm moisture of summer. Before the first frost, go over all the sealed joints in your house, from roof to basement *(pages 16–17)*—even a sealant that is guaranteed for years should get this annual inspection. The spots of greatest danger, and the ones

that most often need recaulking, are the areas around windows and the frames of windows and doors.

Gutters

As the trees shed their leaves, install wire cages at the entrances to downpipes to prevent the pipes from becoming blocked; if necessary, repair or replace existing cages. Later in the season, clean your gutters of fallen leaves and other debris—do not count on rain to move this material, which is likely to mat up and clog your entire rain drainage system. Use a stiff brush to get at dirt and mineral granules washed down from mineral-surfaced roofing; if necessary, dig out encrusted matter at the bottom of a gutter with a small trowel. Finally, flush the gutter out with a garden hose, and cover rust spots with a rust-resistant primer.

Weatherstripping

Like sealants for joins between different construction materials, weatherstripping is usually guaranteed for a period of years but should be inspected annually. The stripping itself may be perfectly sound, but the setting of a house and the friction of a moving sash or door can weaken or destroy the seal. On a windy day, hold a lighted candle near the edges of every weatherstripped window and door to see if there are draughts. Where you discover cracks or defective stripping, thoroughly clean and dry the relevant surfaces and install an appropriate form of new weatherstripping *(pages 8–15)*. If windows do not shut properly, it may be necessary to scrape off dirt and old paint and to sand down their frames; doors that are sagging or swollen may need to be planed or have their hinges reset *(pages 12–13)*.

Window Insulation

If the windows in your house are single glazed, this is a good time to install some form of insulation in preparation for the cold weather of winter. Existing single-glazed windows can be replaced with double or triple-glazed windows; less expensive alternatives include secondary windows attached to the inside of existing casements, or sheets of rigid plastic or plastic film *(pages 94–101)*. Check that all external shutters are in good condition and make any repairs necessary.

Winter

Insulation Check

All walls, ceilings and floors that separate the living areas in your house from the unheated areas should be protected by insulation and an accompanying vapour barrier *(pages 70–73)*. Weak spots in your insulation cover are often hard to detect during the warm months of the year, but may show up clearly when snow blankets your roof. Examine the roof for bare patches or streaks—they are almost certainly above places where the insulation has settled and matted, or where slabs or mats have been pierced or have pulled away from their fastenings. These areas of high heat loss are expensive in terms of fuel costs; repair the insulation immediately. At the same time, check the attic for leaks: melting snow may have penetrated the roof, or old leaks may have soaked the insulation. Roof leaks are difficult to repair in winter, but a bad leak can be so dangerous to the structure of a house that the job of making it good should be undertaken immediately—by a professional, if necessary.

Ice Dams

Despite all precautions, snow may freeze to ice at the edge of a roof, usually starting at a clogged gutter downpipe. Snow builds up above the ice and at the first thaw—or even with the melting caused by a normal heat loss from the roof—melting snow can work its way between the tiles or slates to produce serious leaks. At least once during the winter, check the edges of the roof for ice dams; if you discover any, break them up and remove them.

Termite Check

In warm and tropical regions, termites in their winged stage often swarm in late winter; check the basement for them. Even if you do not see any, take the time for a systematic termite check. Look for small heaps of sawdust on the floor, and for the mud-walled tubes through which termites tunnel towards moisture. To check the interiors of studs and joists, drive a sharp tool—an awl or an ice pick will do—deep into the wood and work it in and out, searching for the small hollows and honeycombed areas that are caused by termite infestation. At any sign of infestation, call in a professional exterminator immediately.

Picture Credits

The sources for the illustrations in this book are shown below. Credits for the pictures from left to right are separated by semicolons, from top to bottom by dashes.

Cover: Martin Brigdale. 6: Martin Brigdale. 8: Drawing by Oxford Illustrators Ltd.; Drawings by Whitman Studio Inc. 9: Drawings by Whitman Studio Inc.—Drawing by Oxford Illustrators Ltd.; Drawings by Whitman Studio Inc. 10–12: Drawings by Oxford Illustrators Ltd. 13: Drawings by Nick Fasciano. 14–17: Drawings by Oxford Illustrators Ltd. 18, 19: Drawings by Peter McGinn. 20: Martin Brigdale. 22–27: Drawings by Oxford Illustrators Ltd. 28: Drawing by Nick Fasciano. 29: Drawings by Whitman Studio Inc. 30, 31: Drawings by Peter McGinn. 32: Drawing by Oxford Illustrators Ltd. 33: Drawing by Oxford Illustrators Ltd.—Drawings by Adolph E. Brotman. 34, 35: Drawings by Oxford Illustrators Ltd. 36: Drawing by Ray Skibinski—Drawings by Oxford Illustrators Ltd. 37–43: Drawings by Oxford Illustrators Ltd. 44: Christine Hinze. 45–47: Drawings by Oxford Illustrators Ltd. 48, 49: Drawings by Ray Skibinski. 50, 51: Drawings by Adolph E. Brotman. 52, 53: Drawings by Nick Fasciano. 54: Drawings by Adolph E. Brotman. 55–57: Drawings by Oxford Illustrators Ltd. 58: Drawing by Vantage Art Inc. 59: Drawings by Edward Vebell. 60: Drawings by Oxford Illustrators Ltd. 61: Drawings by Nick Fasciano. 62–64: Drawings by Oxford Illustrators Ltd. 65: Drawings by Adolph E. Brotman. 66, 67: Drawings by Peter McGinn. 68: Martin Brigdale. 71: Drawings by Vantage Art Inc. 72, 73: Drawing by Oxford Illustrators Ltd. 74: Drawing by Michael Flanagan; Drawing by Oxford Illustrators Ltd. 75: Drawings by Oxford Illustrators Ltd. 76, 77: Drawings by Randall Lieu and Jim Silks. 78: Drawing by Oxford Illustrators Ltd.—Drawings by Vantage Art Inc. 79–81: Drawings by Vantage Art Inc. 82–85: Drawings by Oxford Illustrators Ltd. 86: Drawing by Whitman Studio Inc. 87: Drawing by Oxford Illustrators Ltd.; Drawings by Ray Skibinski—Drawing by Oxford Illustrators Ltd. 88: Drawing by John Sagan—Drawing by Whitman Studio Inc. 89: Drawing by Whitman Studio Inc.—Drawing by Ray Skibinski; Drawing by Whitman Studio Inc. 92–101: Drawings by Oxford Illustrators Ltd. 102: Drawings by Randall Lieu and Jim Silks. 103–107: Drawings by Frederic F. Bigio from B-C Graphics. 108: Drawings by Adolph E. Brotman. 109–110: Drawings by Oxford Illustrators Ltd. 111: Drawings by Adolph E. Brotman. 112: Paul Reeves. 114: Drawing by Oxford Illustrators Ltd. 115: Rentokil, Felcourt, East Grinstead. 116, 117: Drawings by Oxford Illustrators Ltd. 119: Rentokil, Felcourt, East Grinstead. 120, 121: Drawings by Oxford Illustrators Ltd.

Acknowledgements

The editors wish to thank the following: Abru Aluminium Ltd., Launceston; Ace Blinds, London; Aluminium Federation, Birmingham; Association of British Manufacturers of Mineral Insulating Fibres, Bromley; Dave Beadle, Reading; British Chemical Dampcourse Association, Reading; British Gypsum, Gravesend; British Wood Preserving Association, London; Building Research Establishment Advisory Service, Watford; Cement and Concrete Association, London; H.W. Cooper & Co. Ltd., London; Copper Development Association, Potters Bar; Corporate Public Relations Ltd., London; Department of Industry, London; Draughtproofing Advisory Association Ltd., London; Experimental Building Station, Sydney; Tim Fraser, Sydney; Glass and Glazing Federation, London; Aquila Kegan, London; Lead Development Association, London; London Borough of Hammersmith and Fulham, Housing Services, Private Sector; Roy Lucas, Sydney; Marley Extrusions, Maidstone; National Association of Loft Insulation Contractors, London; Nickell's and Co., London; Permablinds Ltd., Dudley; Raven Products Pty. Ltd., Adelaide; Rentokil Ltd., East Grinstead; Vicki Robinson, London; Bob Ryan, Sydney; Sealant Manufacturers Conference, Southampton; Schlegel U.K. Engineering Ltd., London; Timloc Building Products Ltd., Goole; Vent-Axia Ltd., Crawley; Zinc Development Association, London.

Index/Glossary

Metric Conversion Chart

Approximate equivalents—length

Millimetres to inches		Inches to millimetres	
1	1/32	1/32	1
2	1/16	1/16	2
3	1/8	1/8	3
4	5/32	3/16	5
5	3/16	1/4	6
6	1/4	5/16	8
7	9/32	3/8	10
8	5/16	7/16	11
9	11/32	1/2	13
10 (1cm)	3/8	9/16	14
11	7/16	5/8	16
12	15/32	11/16	17
13	1/2	3/4	19
14	9/16	13/16	21
15	19/32	7/8	22
16	5/8	15/16	24
17	11/16	1	25
18	23/32	2	51
19	3/4	3	76
20	25/32	4	102
25	1	5	127
30	13/16	6	152
40	19/16	7	178
50	1 15/16	8	203
60	2 3/8	9	229
70	2 3/4	10	254
80	3 1/8	11	279
90	3 9/16	12 (1ft)	305
100	3 15/16	13	330
200	7 7/8	14	356
300	11 13/16	15	381
400	15 3/4	16	406
500	19 11/16	17	432
600	23 5/8	18	457
700	27 9/16	19	483
800	31 1/2	20	508
900	35 7/16	24 (2ft)	610
1000 (1m)	39 3/8		

Metres to feet/inches		Yards to metres	
		1	0.914
2	6' 7"	2	1.83
3	9' 10"	3	2.74
4	13' 1"	4	3.65
5	16' 5"	5	4.57
6	19' 8"	6	5.49
7	23' 0"	7	6.40
8	26' 3"	8	7.32
9	29' 6"	9	8.23
10	32' 10"	10	9.14
20	65' 7"	20	18.29
50	164' 0"	50	45.72
100	328' 7"	100	91.44

Conversion factors

Length

1 millimetre (mm)	= 0.0394 in
1 centimetre (cm)/10 mm	= 0.3937 in
1 metre/100 cm	= 39.37 in/3.281 ft/1.094 yd
1 kilometre (km)/1000 metres	= 1093.6 yd/0.6214 mile
1 inch (in)	= 25.4 mm/2.54 cm
1 foot (ft)/12 in	= 304.8 mm/30.48 cm/0.3048 metre
1 yard (yd)/3 ft	= 914.4 mm/91.44 cm/0.9144 metre
1 mile/1760 yd	= 1609.344 metres/1.609 km

Area

1 square centimetre (sq cm)/ 100 square millimetres (sq mm)	= 0.155 sq in
1 square metre (sq metre)/10,000 sq cm	= 10.764 sq ft/1.196 sq yd
1 are/100 sq metres	= 119.60 sq yd/0.0247 acre
1 hectare (ha)/100 ares	= 2.471 acres/0.00386 sq mile
1 square inch (sq in)	= 645.16 sq mm/6.4516 sq cm
1 square foot (sq ft)/144 sq in	= 929.03 sq cm
1 square yard (sq yd)/9 sq ft	= 8361.3 sq cm/0.8361 sq metre
1 acre/4840 sq yd	= 4046.9 sq metres/0.4047 ha
1 square mile/640 acres	= 259 ha/2.59 sq km

Volume

1 cubic centimetre (cu cm)/ 1000 cubic millimetres (cu mm)	= 0.0610 cu in
1 cubic decimetre (cu dm)/1000 cu cm	= 61.024 cu in/0.0353 cu ft
1 cubic metre/1000 cu dm	= 35.3146 cu ft/1.308 cu yd
1 cu cm	= 1 millilitre (ml)
1 cu dm	= 1 litre see **Capacity**
1 cubic inch (cu in)	= 16.3871 cu cm
1 cubic foot (cu ft)/1728 cu in	= 28.3168 cu cm/0·0283 cu metre
1 cubic yard (cu yd)/27 cu ft	= 0.7646 cu metre

Capacity

1 litre	= 1.7598 pt/0.8799 qt/0.22 gal
1 pint (pt)	= 0.568 litre
1 quart (qt)	= 1.137 litres
1 gallon (gal)	= 4.546 litres

Weight

1 gram (g)	= 0.035 oz
1 kilogram (kg)/1000 g	= 2.20 lb/35.2 oz
1 tonne/1000 kg	= 2204.6 lb/0.9842 ton
1 ounce (oz)	= 28.35 g
1 pound (lb)	= 0.4536 kg
1 ton	= 1016 kg

Pressure

1 gram per square metre (g/metre^2)	= 0.0292 oz/sq yd
1 gram per square centimetre (g/cm^2)	= 0.226 oz/sq in
1 kilogram per square centimetre (kg/cm^2)	= 14.226 lb/sq in
1 kilogram per square metre (kg/metre^2)	= 0.205 lb/sq ft
1 pound per square foot (lb/ft^2)	= 4.882 kg/metre^2
1 pound per square inch (lb/in^2)	= 703.07 kg/metre^2
1 ounce per square yard (oz/yd^2)	= 33.91 g/metre^2
1 ounce per square foot (oz/ft^2)	= 305.15 g/metre^2

Temperature

To convert °F to °C, subtract 32, then divide by 9 and multiply by 5

To convert °C to °F, divide by 5 and multiply by 9, then add 32

Phototypeset by Tradespools Limited, Frome, Somerset
Printed in Spain by Artes Gráficas Toledo, S.A.
D. L. TO: 1182 -1984